C L A S S I C
CONVERTIBLES

CLASSIC
CONVERTIBLES

NICKY WRIGHT

MetroBooks

MetroBooks

An Imprint of Friedman/Fairfax Publishers

Library of Congress Cataloging–in–Publication Data

Wright, Nicky.

   Classic convertibles / Nicky Wright.

      p. cm.

   Includes index.

   ISBN 1-56799-432-6

   1. Automobiles, Convertible—United States—History. I. Title.

TI23.W755 1997

338.4'7629222—dc21   96-40508

Editor: Tony Burgess
Art Director: Jeff Batzli
Designers: Meredith Miller and Garrett Schuh
Photography Editor: Christopher C. Bain
Production Manager: Camille Lee

Color separations by Ocean Graphic International Company
Printed in China by Leefung-Asco Printers Ltd.

1 3 5 7 9 10 8 6 4 2

For bulk purchases and special sales, please contact:
Friedman/Fairfax Publishers
Attention: Sales Department
15 West 26th Street
New York, NY 10010
212/685-6610 FAX 212/685-1307

Visit our website:
http://www.metrobooks.com

DEDICATION:

To all my good friends and family in England, thank you.

ACKNOWLEDGMENTS:

The following people and institutions helped me immeasurably in the creation of this book:
Auburn-Cord-Duesenberg Museum, Auburn, Indiana; Deer Park Auto Museum, Escondido,
California; Gilmore Classic Car Museum, Kalamazoo, Michigan; National Auto Museum,
Reno, Nevada; Prairie Door Auto, La Porte, Indiana; Chrysler Corporation; General Motors
Corporation, Pontiac Motor Division; Chrysler Jeep, Dover, Kent, England; Classic Heaven,
Arizona; Tom and Karen Barnes; Russ Bell; Don Bergman; John Buchannan; Mike Barron and
Luis Corona; Dick Choler; William J. Chorkey; Ron Columbo and Keya Costianes;
Duke Davenport; William Goodsene; Blaine Jenkins; Pete Kesling; Elliot Klein; Robert Knapp;
Bud and Bonita Lilley; Robert Lutz; Bob and Colleen Mason; Glen Patch; Bob Schmidt;
and the owners of the 1964 Lincoln Continental, 1965 Chevrolet Caprice, and 1959 Cadillac.

CONTENTS

INTRODUCTION

The sun is out, the sky is blue, and the road ahead is arrow-straight. You sit back, the wind whipping through your hair. You peer through the windshield and inhale the sweet, clear air into your lungs. Ahead of you, under the long, sweeping hood, the familiar burble of a contented V8 moves you onward, ever onward, to wherever your fancy takes you.

Then you wake up! You're in your armchair and you have fallen asleep briefly. A car magazine is on your lap, the pages turned to an article about a convertible rather like the one you remember your father's neighbor owning many years ago. Remember how you loved that car, with its shiny chrome, big fins, and two-tone paint. "One day," you had said to yourself, "I'll have one of those, and when I do, I shall drive into the sunset, forever fancy-free."

Convertible automobiles have always represented freedom and wide-open spaces. Although the first cars were made in Europe, convertibles were a distinctly American phenomenon. They arrived on the scene in 1927 and have been with us ever since.

A convertible is a car possessing a top that is permanently attached to the frame and that may be lifted and lowered either by hand or, as is more common, mechanically at the touch of a button. In essence, it is a hardtop with the roof sliced off and extra strength given to the body to prevent flexing and distortion. The doors have power or manual windows that fit snugly into the top when it is up and give protection from the elements if it is down. Though many of the earliest cars were open, they were not strictly convertibles. Once open, always open so not really "convertible" from one type of car to another. Dual-cowl phaetons had canvas tops, but lacked windows. Then there were the old "surrey with a fringe on top" cars of the late 1890s, the dashing British roadsters and sports cars of the 1930s, all open cars with romantic appeal. But they weren't true convertibles.

It has been many years since America was introduced to the first seven cars that were truly convertibles. From that day on, the convertible has become an intrinsic part of motoring folklore, a dream machine tinged with romance, wide open spaces, and hair blown by a dancing wind. Through thick and thin, the convertible has emerged unscathed, a little wiser, a little safer, but still a car meant for sunny days and warm nights. Here then, is the story of the romantic legend that is the convertible. Drop that top and away we go!

Chapter 1

ESCAPE ROAD ROMANCE

I t was 1927 and the United States was enjoying the good life. There was nearly full employment, the stock market was buoyant, and Americans had the highest standard of living in the nation's history. Thirty-nine percent of the world's automobiles were owned by U.S. citizens; statistics show that nine million cars were registered in the United States, one for every six people. Wall Street applauded when General Motors (GM) declared the biggest dividend in the country's history. The 17.4 million shares of stock realized a payout of $65,250,000! All things considered, 1927 was a good year for the motor industry, and the convertible was 1927's main claim to automotive fame.

PRECEDING PAGES: The elegant 1932 Chrysler Custom Imperial CL convertible, with body work by LeBaron and a 384.8 cubic inch (6306 cubic cm) straight 8 engine, was one of the finest Chryslers ever made.

Open cars had been around since 1886, when the first one, a three-wheeled Benz, sputtered down a German dirt road. (In fact, that first Benz had no roof at all, and not much else besides.) Many former coach-makers turned to building automobiles, some making custom bodies for various expensive car chassis. Few realized it at the time, but they were witnessing the birth of a social revolution that would transform the world.

For the most part, the early cars were of simple construction, and, for the first fifteen years or so, they were generally of open design. Soon, canvas tops arrived on the scene, along with some very decorative surreys complete with fringes, and odd little cars like the 1909 British Pearson-Cox Model F steam car with a top best described as a giant cockleshell, fitting over a very sloping windshield. As for two-seater roadsters, forget it. You just didn't get a top!

It didn't take long to recognize the romance attached to driving an open car. America was wide open ninety years ago, with big, empty spaces

that Edward "Ned" Jordan immortalized in his emotionally appealing advertisements for his famous Playboy cars. A two-seater open roadster with a canvas top to protect against the elements, the Jordan Playboy was the first car to emphasize free-as-the-wind, open-air motoring. Jordan, the owner and driving force behind his successful concern, The Jordan Motor Company, was a very talented copywriter. His 1923 ode, "Somewhere West of Laramie," has become the most famous automobile advertisement of all time. It was most definitely responsible for the huge sales success the Playboy had.

By 1916, when the first Jordan appeared, World War I was raging in Europe. America hadn't yet joined the conflict, and this gave American car manufacturers the chance to jump ahead of their European counterparts, whose factories had turned from automobiles to mechanized war machines. By the teen years, cars had begun to rid themselves of the carriage look. People were intrigued by the new designs, the V8 engines, the self-starters (a Cadillac innovation), the hydraulic brakes, the electric windshield wipers, and much more. The U.S. auto industry was on a roll, with new companies springing up on almost a weekly basis—and going under at about the same rate. Soon it became difficult to

ABOVE: *The mighty Duesenberg J, an Indiana-built car, sported a whopping DOHC straight eight that developed 265 bhp. This 1929 example is a Dual-Cowl Phaeton, which means it has two windshields. But it has no side windows, only curtains.*

ABOVE RIGHT: *As befitting a car of Duesenberg's stature, only the very best materials were used in its construction. A somewhat optimistic 150 mph speedometer was part of the comprehensive instrumentation set in a beautiful panel of engine-turned oxidized nickel.*

Another view of the splendid Duesenberg Convertible Coupé. Although other coach-builders tried their hand at convertible coupés, Murphy's were by far the most popular. Note the movable hand-built trunk at the rear.

discern exactly how many different marques had appeared since 1896. Recently, with a pen, paper, and calculator, somebody figured out that more than four thousand different marques had been produced in America in the last hundred years. That is staggering compared to the far smaller number left today.

On April 6, 1917, America finally entered the Great War, and the American auto industry switched to war production. But it was a short interruption: eighteen months later, on November 11, 1918, World War I ended. Car production resumed at full pace, with the popular Ford Model T leading the way into a new age—even though it hadn't advanced much from its birth in 1909.

Not that anybody worried: more than any other car, the Model T put the world on wheels, and opened new horizons for those who had never traveled much farther than their local church. Motoring was advancing by leaps and bounds. In 1920, engineering geniuses Frederick and August Duesenberg put hydraulic brakes on their cars, technology that would be copied by Chrysler in 1924. Duesenberg cars also boasted overhead cam

engines, the result of experience gained on the race tracks. Later on, Duesenberg made sporty convertibles fit for a king—and it was frequently kings who would buy them! The fun years were 1920 to 1928, when the Jazz Age was in full swing and flamboyance was the norm. Everything was booming on the car front, with many of the smaller makes doing particularly well.

As nobody really knows who invented the convertible, it has been assumed it was a collective idea. We do know that 1927 was the first year a convertible appeared in the showrooms of eight different car-makers: Buick, Cadillac-LaSalle, DuPont, Lincoln, Chrysler, Stearns, Whippet, and Willys, the latter three all under the John Willys umbrella. Cadillac's entry was perhaps the most significant, for it gave birth to a new marque that was the direct result of GM's brand-new art and color studio headed by a very tall thirty-year-old named Harley Earl.

Earl was born in 1893, the son of a Hollywood coach-builder who ran a successful wagon- and carriage-making business. When automobiles came into their own, J.W. Earl's business switched to bolt-on car acces-

sories, then complete, custom-made bodies. It was at his father's works that Harley Earl received his baptism in the art of designing automobile bodies. Hollywood was establishing itself as the movie capital of the world, and the screen stars it created became regular customers at the Earl Automobile Company. As time went on, Harley was designing custom car bodies for Tom Mix and Fatty Arbuckle, along with other celebrities. In 1919, one of Earl's best customers, the Don Lee West Coast Cadillac distributor, bought the company, including Earl, whose car designs were attracting a lot of attention from not only the rich and famous, but also from high-powered motoring executives at General Motors.

One of those executives, Lawrence P. Fisher, president of Cadillac Motor Division, was much taken with Harley Earl's work on the occasions he saw it at Don Lee. A flamboyant extrovert, Fisher realized how boring contemporary car shapes were and felt that a new design approach would have to be considered. General Motors chairman Alfred Sloan agreed, and Earl was soon hired to create and manage the world's first car company design studio.

ABOVE: *George Pierce began the Pierce-Arrow company in 1901 with the 2 ¾ horsepower Motorette. By 1913, Pierce-Arrow was an established luxury car-maker, and it was in this year that the first pod-like headlamps appeared. Optional in the beginning, the flared into fender lamps became Pierce-Arrow's trademark.*

ABOVE RIGHT: *Evolved from Duesenberg's SOHC racing engine, this beautiful DOHC straight-eight was state-of-the-art in 1929. The cylinder block was painted green enamel, the exhaust pipe in heat-proof green enamel. Other visible parts were either chrome-plated or polished aluminum.*

LEFT: *Duesenbergs, like fine tailored suits, were made to order. This smart 1929 Model J was one of 55 Convertible Coupés, or Roadsters, put together by coach-builder Murphy.*

Christened the Art & Color Section, a name Earl considered "sissy," the studio revolutionized car thinking forever. In March 1927, GM introduced an entirely new car: the LaSalle. It was sold under the Cadillac banner and was designed to fit in between the most expensive Buick and the cheapest Cadillac. Although it was less costly than its more illustrious cousins, the mere fact that it was in the Cadillac fold

would attract those wanting Caddie style without paying the required premium. The LaSalle was offered in the usual range of models, including one that had never been attempted until 1927—a convertible.

The Cadillac division wasn't the only company offering convertibles that year; as noted earlier, seven other car manufacturers had had the same idea, though no doubt for entirely different reasons. There was little question in anybody's mind that the LaSalle was a most handsome automobile. This five-passenger sedan still retained the boxy look prevalent throughout the industry, but with a difference: it was no longer a series of boxes mounted one on top of the other, but a cohesive shape accentuated by softly rounded curves where before there had only been sharp corners. The lowered silhouette featured in all 1927 LaSalle models became something of an Earl trademark, and was shortly copied by everyone else in the industry.

It seemed to be the ideal car, one that could be open or closed depending on the weather. Of course, it was always advisable to check the skies before embarking upon an open adventure into the country. Cloudbursts can happen suddenly, and it was no fun for driver and passenger to wrestle with a top in the pouring rain. All things considered, GM's LaSalle was the handsomest of the eight convertibles announced in 1927. It had the flair and panache of high style, and fit very well into the restless, progressive mode of the time. The roof folded by means of chrome-plated landau irons, coming to rest behind the rear seat. A canvas boot protected the top when it was down. Beautifully made, the LaSalle was a worthy addition to the Cadillac line. But even though the LaSalle stole the honors for styling excellence, the other seven convertibles were also very attractive.

Three of the others, the Stearns, Whippet, and Willys, came from the same stable. Ford made a convertible out of its luxury Brunn-bodied Lincoln. Not to be outdone, relative newcomer Chrysler started its Imperial 80 series with a smart convertible costing $3,495. That was quite expensive considering Buick's Master Six hit the road at a mere $1,925. If the LaSalle was the result of new design thinking, then the DuPont can't have been far behind. E. Paul du Pont was a man very much abreast of contemporary ideas, as his quality-built cars proved. To own a DuPont

was to own something special; from du Pont's first car in 1920 to the last in 1932, production was limited to a scant 537 vehicles over the twelve-year period. Mention du Pont in collectors' circles today and immediately people think of the Model G Speedster or convertible. Here was high style without the benefit of an art and color studio like GM's, though many of the cars were given custom coachwork.

One of the most attractive DuPont convertibles was the 1929 Model G with a body by Merrimac. Interesting features were the body-colored rounded grille and wire mesh chrome wheels. As noted earlier, by the late twenties, America's most popular cars were the closed-body types; nonetheless, the new convertibles struck a chord in the hearts of many

who liked, but couldn't afford, them. In 1928, a Chrysler Series 72 Rumble Seat Coupé sold 6,869 units, compared to the Series 72 convertible, which sold 1,729. The convertible total looks much smaller if one adds the total production for the other six closed-body styles available. Still, the convertible caught on; fifteen car-makers had them by 1928.

Packard, christened "America's Rolls-Royce" by British motoring scribes, had three convertibles in 1928, thus eclipsing luxury rivals Cadillac and Lincoln. Franklin introduced its Airman 3/5 passenger convertible, and Graham-Paige had four, beginning with the Senior Six at $2,185. Graham's most expensive offering was the Model 835 Eight, costing $2,485. Auburn offered its first convertible in 1928, after entrepreneur Erret Lobban Cord took over the

Judging by the number of expensive luxury cars built in 1932, one would never think the United States was reeling under the worst economic depression ever known. Maybe the auto industry was trying to maintain a positive outlook by making beautiful cars, like this Chrysler Custom Imperial CL Convertible Coupé by LeBaron. Actually, only 28 of this model were built in 1932.

ailing company; sales promptly zoomed. Peerless, Nash, Studebaker, and Auburn all had convertibles in 1928, the revitalized Auburn fielding five, ranging from the economy 6-66 to the big straight-eight 115 model. Besides moving its standard 80 Series convertible to the lower-priced 72 Series, Chrysler also offered two custom-bodied convertibles in 1928. These were long-wheelbase, top-of-the-line Imperials in the 80 Series: a LeBaron 2/4 passenger and a Dietrich convertible sedan. Very few were actually built; thirty-nine LeBarons at $3,995, and ten Dietrich models at $6,485. Some sources claim that only four of the latter were built; the true total is probably somewhere in between. Whatever the actual number, their scarcity makes them valuable collectibles.

But the big news in the automotive world was the merger of Chrysler and Dodge Brothers. At the time, Dodge was a much bigger concern than Chrysler, which had come about with Walter P. Chrysler's acquisition of Maxwell in 1922. Anyway, the Chrysler takeover of Dodge was described at the time as "a minnow swallowing a whale." The deal proved very successful, giving birth to both DeSoto and Plymouth in the same year. The merger catapulted Chrysler to the number three spot behind GM and Ford, a position the company hasn't relinquished since.

Nineteen-twenty-eight was a boom year. Stocks on Wall Street hit record highs, and Herbert Hoover accepted the Republican presidential nomination with the slogan "A chicken in every pot, a car in every garage." Car sales were much the same as in 1927, though Chevrolet wouldn't agree, having dropped from 1,749,998 in 1927 to 888,050 in 1928. Ford doubled its production over the same period. Car sales were mixed in 1929, even though Dodge, Hupmobile, and Pontiac/Oakland joined the growing convertible club. Mechanical and design innovations introduced on closed cars were standard on convertibles as well, and in 1929 Dodge came out with automatic windshield wipers, brake lights, and the first downdraft carburetor fitted to an American car. Over at GM, Cadillac's junior, the LaSalle, was joined by baby cousins, the Viking from Oldsmobile and the Marquette from Buick. Oakland celebrated its fifteenth anniversary in 1925 with the birth of Pontiac.

These smaller, lighter, and cheaper cars were the result of GM chairman Alfred Sloan's belief that every price slot should be covered, lest a competitor get ahead of the General. As time would shortly tell, theory doesn't necessarily work in practice. In a turnabout that wasn't really meant, Pontiac was outselling its parent, eight to one, by 1929!

On March 17, David Dunbar Buick, inventor of enamel baths and maker of the car bearing his name, passed away. Although his Buick was a great success, and is one of the oldest surviving cars in existence, Buick himself died penniless and alone. A couple of weeks later, on April 4, Carl Benz, the man who changed the world with his invention of the automobile, died at the age of 84. After years of carefree living, 1929 contained portents suggesting that all was not well. People didn't take much notice, for they were caught in a frenzied stock-buying spree that seemed as though it might never end. But it did end, with calamitous results, on October 24, 1929.

In hours of frantic selling, fortunes were lost, companies died on pieces of paper, and the biggest financial debacle the world had ever seen enveloped the globe. The Great Depression had begun. Before the crash, Pontiac had introduced its new line of cars. Called the "New Big Six," in reference to the larger-capacity in-line six-cylinder engine, Pontiac had several body styles, including its first convertible. This was a rumble seat cabriolet upholstered in exotic mohair. Neatly applied trim striping helped add luster to this $845 car that looked as though it cost a great deal more. Sales of more than 188,000 were very good despite the economic gloom, but would Pontiac and the rest of the auto industry be able to sustain the numbers they were accustomed to?

Sales might have been in doubt, but ingenuity was still up. Front-wheel drive was a new concept as far as American car manufacturers were concerned, but when Harry Miller pioneered it in America with his series of successful racing cars (the first of which placed second in the 1926 Indianapolis 500), auto entrepreneurs Archie Andrews and Erret Lobban Cord were much impressed with the racers and the extremely low profile that front-wheel drive gave the cars. It was obvious to the two that front-wheel drive was the wave of the future, and, being the compulsive whiz kids they were, Andrews and Cord decided to pitch their all into developing front-wheel drive immediately.

Cord beat Andrews, who founded the ill-fated Ruxton, by acquiring the patent rights to Miller's front-wheel drive racing transaxle and taking on Miller as a consultant. Another consultant Cord hired was racing driver (and friend) Leon Duray, who told Cord that Miller's transaxle wouldn't work in a

ABOVE: *Viewed from the side, this 1931 Cadillac Model 452A All-Weather Phaeton has a more sedate appearance than many of its contemporaries. Not as fleet as the Imperial, not as racy as the Duesenberg, Cadillac's formality was a great sales point.*

TOP: *Cadillac had several windshield variations in the early 1930s, this two piece V-shaped design being one of them. Along with the large radiator grille, the split windshield tended to give Cadillacs a rather armor-plated look.*

street car, partly because of the highly stressed racing gears. Instead, Duray insisted, try Cornelius Willett Van Ranst's front-wheel drive setup built for another of Miller's racing models. It was a more robust, simpler unit, which, with development, would be ideal for passenger vehicles. Taking Duray's advice, Cord hired Van Ranst to take charge of the development of his front-wheel drive system for the L-29.

In 1929, the front-wheel drive Cord L-29 and Ruxton were launched. Both cars had low profiles and long hoods; Al Leamy (a creative artist in

the Harley Earl mold) was responsible for the design of the Cord L-29, which was far better looking than the rather top-heavy Ruxton. In fact, Leamy's lovely convertible helped the Cord win thirty-nine

prizes for style, beauty, and engineering innovation across Europe. Convertible versions of both cars were stunning, although the same couldn't be said for their somewhat lackluster mechanical abilities.

Unfortunately, through no fault of their own, the Cord and Ruxton managements couldn't have picked a worse time to debut their striking new cars. Launching an all-new car like the Cord in 1929 was very bad timing—especially if the car was to be the most expensive automobile ever built in America. Both cars were priced at a little over $3,000 (a lot of money when one could buy a Chrysler Roadster for as little as $885 or a Ford Model A Phaeton for not much more than $400). When Ruxton went under in 1930, it left the front-wheel drive arena to Cord, whose L-29 had its own share of troubles. Still, Cord persevered with the L-29 until 1932, when it was withdrawn following problems and complaints that it was worse than useless on fairly steep gradients. But Cord wasn't about to give up his namesake, so it was back to the drawing board for the engineers. Although front-wheel drive was a revolution in American car design, a smaller, yet even more important one was taking place.

The Duesenberg brothers, better at making cars than money, had been saved from ruin in 1925, when Cord bought their company. A new, revitalized Duesenberg hit the roads in 1929. It was, as Erret Lobban Cord had requested of the Duesenberg brothers, the finest automobile in the world. It was far more advanced than a Rolls-Royce, albeit not as smooth

or as comfortable. The Duesenbergs brushed criticisms aside airily. After all, the Duesenbergs' engine was a race-bred, dual overhead cam straight-eight developing a massive 265 horsepower and boasting a top speed well in excess of 100 mph (160kph). Naturally, with a car costing upward of $13,000 in 1929, there were convertible models as well. Of the 470 or 480 Duesenberg Js and SJs built, most had custom bodies. When you bought a car as expensive as a Duesenberg, you wanted it to be unique. Therefore, customers ordered their own bodywork, be it a closed sedan, phaeton, or convertible, from the plethora of coach-builders eager to do their bidding. Possibly because they built the handsomest ones, Murphy Coachbuilders of Pasadena, California, created the majority of convertibles. Many of their convertibles were styled by the legendary Franklin Hershey, although he is probably better known for putting the chrome stripes on Pontiac's hood and helping to create the 1955 Thunderbird.

There really wasn't much to touch the Duesenberg J when it was introduced in December 1928 for the 1929 model year. Mounted on a whopping 141-inch (358.1cm) wheelbase, or the even larger 153-inch (388.6cm) wheelbase—both were standard—Duesenbergs could be as flamboyant or as modest as the customer liked. Thankfully, most takers veered toward tasteful flamboyance without the baroque associated with certain ultra-expensive, very low-production European makes of the day.

No matter how good the Duesenberg was, it didn't strike a chord

with old money as much as it did with new. Duesenbergs certainly won the hearts of Hollywood, though: Clark Gable, Gary Cooper, Greta Garbo, and Mae West were among the stars seen driving Sunset Boulevard in Duesenbergs. Both Cooper and Gable had convertibles; later, each

ordered an identical short-wheelbase, supercharged roadster. Called the SSJ, these were the only two of their kind ever built.

At the other end of the motoring spectrum, there was Studebaker's little Erskine. It had a 108-inch (274.3cm) wheelbase and came in various body styles, including a smart two-passenger convertible. The Erskine was

One of the most striking convertible designs is the 1931 Duesenberg J Convertible Victoria by Rollston. The raked windshield, long, flowing front fenders and low roof line blend into a cohesive whole. Here is a car that sums up the Great Gatsby generation: rich, elegant, and irresponsibly free.

an inexpensive compact car that should have sold well during the Depression years but didn't. It faded away in 1930.

Auto manufacturers were looking closely at Harley Earl and GM's innovative Art & Color Studio. Some, like Cord, realized the importance of car stylists. He hired Al Leamy, then, a little later, Gordon Buehrig, who, more than any other designer, elevated car design to a twentieth-century art form. Apart from the opinionated Henry Ford, who said of car styling that he did not care five cents for all the art the world had ever produced, most companies were falling over themselves to hire car designers. Stiff competition and an "I-told-you-so" attitude forced Ford to reconsider his somewhat rash beliefs, with the result that Ford soon had a design team to compete with other manufacturers.

In terms of design, Cadillac relied almost exclusively for its swish coachwork on GM's in-house coach-builder, Fisher, with some work also

done by Fleetwood. Between 1930 and 1931, 3,250 V16 Cadillacs were built, of which 211 were the beautiful convertible coupé. None, as far as is known, were styled by Harley Earl, who was getting over his 1929 "Pregnant Buick" failure, a car designed with bulging sides and more rounded lines than were usual at the time. The 1930–32 designs were handled by GM coach-builders Fisher or Fleetwood for the most part, with Fisher doing the majority of cars. Cadillac convertible coupés were beautiful machines, irrespective of the power plant beneath the hood. Obviously, the most common was the V8, followed by the V12 and then the V16. Even if a V8 convertible looked the same as a V16 model, the engine designation emblem on the headlight crossbar immediately identified which type it was.

One of the oddest anomalies that occurred during the first three years of the Depression was the debut appearance of a number of multicylinder luxury cars that were the nectar of power and wealth. There was the ultra-powerful Duesenberg, all four valves per cylinder of it; the stunning V12 and V16 Cadillacs; a relatively inexpensive Auburn V12 with twelve cylinders; a striking new car from Pierce-Arrow (only seven Silver Arrows were built, but none were convertibles); and then two more sixteen-cylinder behemoths from Marmon and Peerless. Many of the nouveaux riche had lost everything (including their shirts) when Wall Street collapsed; only old money managed to pull through reasonably unscathed, and it was these folks that Cadillac, Packard, Pierce-Arrow, and Marmon wanted to keep happy. After all, it was the rich who would buy a multicylinder car, if they bought one at all.

Perhaps the one car designed specifically for old money was the Packard. From its beginnings in 1899, Packard's name was synonymous with elegance, grace, quality, and good taste. Cadillac was especially envious; with two Dewar trophies to its name, Cadillac felt the king of the hill honor really belonged to the "Standard of the World," so-called after the company won the first Dewar Trophy in 1907. Obviously, the wealthy didn't agree; Packard outsold Cadillac an average of two to one until 1934, then by a lot more until 1939, when Cadillac finally took over. Solid, well-made cars that they were, Packard's square and rather stodgy styling up to 1929 was nothing to write home about. In 1930, styles began to change: the cars were lower, and the convertibles

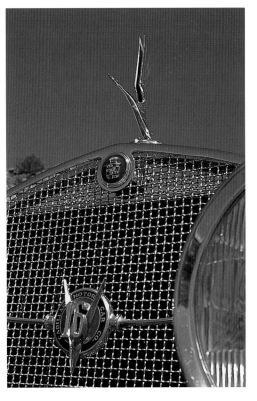

began to look sleek, especially those bodied by outside coach-builders. Remember, there were four convertible types: the convertible coupé, convertible sedan, convertible victoria, and convertible cabriolet. Packard had them all, but so did everyone else, including down-market Ford.

Ford was truly amazing and his company revolutionary, for a time, but this changed as he grew older and more conservative. In 1926, Ford introduced the five-day week for six days' pay and raised wages to a staggering $7 a day after the stock market crashed. (At least Ford employees did all right during the early part of the Depression.) Chevrolet had brought out its first convertible sports cabriolet in 1929, and Ford was quick to follow with its own convertible in 1929. In fact, if it hadn't been for the changeover from Model T to Model A, there's every likelihood Ford would have had one at the same time as Chevrolet. Not that it mattered much; Ford led Chevrolet by almost two to one in 1929. Out of eighteen different body types, there was only one true convertible: a con-

vertible cabriolet. Of the 1,967,741 Fords produced in 1929, 16,421 were convertible cabriolets, while roadsters accounted for 191,529 units (both figures are for 1929 calendar year production).

At a price of $670, the little Model A convertible cabriolet (in two- and four-passenger models) was no Duesenberg, but it meant everyone could enjoy open-air motoring with the advantage of a well-fitted top and roll-up windows. Thus, it was a bit surprising to find convertibles, especially cute little Ford convertibles, not selling as well as they might. The reason was simple: the roadster cost $200 less—so who needed roll-up windows? Even in the market of the wealthy, convertibles sold in limited numbers. There were 213 V16 Cadillac convertibles of all types sold out of a total 3,250 in 1930 and 1931. This was a slightly higher percentage of convertible sales than Ford had, but it was still disappointing. Roadsters, on the other hand, were commanding high numbers, though tourers were virtually extinct.

But, by the mid-thirties, roadsters too would be an extinct species, with the phaeton holding on a little longer. And by the end of the thirties, the convertible would be the only open car available, thus making the romance of open-air motoring that much more inviting and mysterious. Besides the number of convertibles—there were open-air cars for every budget—there were no encouraging signs from the car-makers. As the Depression dug in its heels, car sales dropped alarmingly. Ford went from nearly two million in 1929 to a little more than one million, Chevrolet crashed from 1,238,605 to 647,520, and everyone else's sales dropped by fifty percent or more. This was not a good time to sell convertibles. Many of the very rich didn't want to be seen as flamboyant or ruffle any feathers during this trying time when ordinary people could not afford new cars at all. If anything, the Depression hastened political change for the worse in many countries; but while peace reigned, America bought cars, though nowhere near as many as in the bonanza years.

In a sense, convertibles came about at precisely the wrong time, but even so, there were seventeen different marques offering convertibles in 1930, the year the Depression really took hold of the nation. President Hoover claimed America was better off than other countries—a message that didn't exactly strike a chord in the hearts of the millions waiting in breadlines.

A number of car-makers died in 1930. Motor corporations with shattered dreams joined the long line of bankruptcies. Some companies killed off unprofitable models: Studebaker got rid of Erskine, Oldsmobile ended Viking's short life. Kissel was on its last legs, and Moon, the car Erret Lobban Cord used to sell so successfully, went under, as did Ruxton.

ABOVE: *Birds, along with the female form, were popular hood ornament designs. Packard had the Cormorant, Duesenberg the "Duesenbird," and Cadillac the Heron. Cadillac offered two hood ornaments through 1932; the other was the popular goddess that became standard as the thirties progressed.*

Chapter 2

SUCCESSES AND FAILURES

By 1930, Oldsmobile's sad little Viking had gone, like others, heavenward. It was a shame, because the Viking convertible was a handsome six-cylinder car. Unfortunately, it couldn't have come along at a worse possible time. In fact, nothing that was new could be sold to the desperate millions whose first thought was survival.

However, GM, Ford, and Chrysler were strong enough to withstand the Depression. Even Packard, Hudson, Nash, and several others survived. But many independent companies didn't make it. It was a razor's edge situation for famous names such as Marmon, Pierce-Arrow, and the Cord empire. Still, they gritted their corporate

over from roadsters and tourers, which, along with phaetons, had an 83 percent market share in 1920. By 1931, sales of all types of open cars had dropped to around three percent; closed coupés and sedans commanded a huge 97 percent. Nineteen-thirty-one saw the last Chrysler roadsters and tourers; the following year it was convertibles only. A few concerns hung on to roadsters, phaetons, and tourers, but the writing was on the wall. By 1940, even the phaeton was gone. Selling any type of car in 1931 was a chore, and convertibles, which were fast becoming the top-of-the-line in any model series, were the hardest hit.

Even so, ultraexpensive convertibles continued to appear in 1932, a year in which the blight on America's workforce continued unabated. In November, Franklin D. Roosevelt was elected president; his New Deal helped in no small way to bring America back from the brink. With the new administration and new president, there was a glimmer of hope across the land. Roosevelt didn't waste time before enacting legislation to put America back to work, signing the radical National Recovery Administration into law. The NRA, the President said, was going to "put people back to work." This it did; more than 1.6 million jobs were created in a three-month period. Wall Street showed its optimism by making its best gains in years, and the country's hope was soon reflected in car sales, which began to climb back after 1933. Convertibles began to sell again, though in relatively small numbers.

Stutz, of Indianapolis, Indiana, had had a fair run since its 1911 beginnings but was suffering in the 1930s. Nevertheless, the company persevered, bringing out the superb DV (dual valve) 32 models. This was Stutz's answer to the multicylindered Cadillacs, Packards, and Marmons, and, in many ways, it was a far more advanced car. It had twin overhead camshafts and four valves per cylinder, with horsepower ranging from 113 to 156, depending on the model. Even though Stutz sold only 421 cars in 1931, the array of models for 1932 made Cadillac look like a nonstarter!

That year there were at least four different five-passenger convertibles built on a 145-inch (368.3cm) or 134-inch (340.3cm) wheelbase. A number of the body styles, including convertibles, were custom built by

teeth and went on producing cars that were not only beautiful but technologically advanced as well.

For sheer head-turning good looks, Chrysler's 1931 Imperial CG convertible has to be one of the best. The General's pioneering of a stylist's studio prompted everyone else to follow suit. Chrysler had Herb Weissinger, who looked at Leamy's Cord, then copied its low profile—though he did add a few ideas of his own. Nowadays Weissinger would be sued for plagiarism; in 1930, people were more gentlemanly in their dealings, and Cord probably took comfort in the fact that "imitation is the sincerest form of flattery." Nonetheless, the Imperial and Chrysler's CD convertibles were attractive cars, and at least they drove satisfactorily; after all, Chrysler stuck to front engine, rear drive. Cord was still having problems with Van Ranst's front-wheel drive system. The car was slow on the straight, hopeless on hills.

As 1931 wore on, the Great Depression grew steadily worse. On the car front, everybody had convertibles to offer and they were rapidly taking

Weymann or LeBaron. One of the prettiest was the 1933 DV32 convertible coupé, which was as nimble as it was fast. Unfortunately, this thoroughbred car died in January 1935 after having sold only six—yes, six—cars in 1934. Another great classic, the beautiful Marmon, ended a thirty-one-year record of excellence in 1933. Four years later, the mighty Duesenberg, arguably the greatest car-maker in the world, closed up shop. Over a four-year period, three of the world's finest automakers died—and coincidentally they all came from Indianapolis.

Although it wasn't record-breaking, there was a marked sales increase in the more popularly priced cars, such as Ford, Chevrolet, Plymouth, and Hudson. Unfortunately, even with its striking twelve-cylinder models, Auburn's sales slide continued, and there was no letup yet for Packard, Cadillac, Lincoln, and others from the top drawer. Dodge had no fewer than three convertibles in 1933, including an eight-cylinder convertible sedan. Despite the fact that Dodge sold three times as many cars in 1933 as it did in 1932, convertible sales accounted for a mere 1,658 units. Because only ninety-five convertibles were eight-cylinder models, Dodge dropped them, leaving only a six-cylinder convertible coupé model for 1934. For the second straight year, Dodge sales increased, but convertible sales dropped 250 units in 1934.

Although Packard lost a couple of thousand units in 1933, the company produced perhaps the most beautiful convertible to be made in what is now regarded as the classic era. There were other great cars, such as the freshly designed Cadillac, Duesenberg SJ, and big Buick 88C, but there was nothing to touch the simplicity of line and the sheer elegance of the Packard Convertible Victoria bodied by Dietrich.

Raymond Henri Dietrich was a designer extraordinaire. He began as an apprentice draftsman with Brewster & Company, coach-builders of New York. Brewster was famous for its American Rolls-Royce coachwork, but custom bodies were fitted to Marmon and Packard as well. Leaving Brewster, Dietrich went on to form LeBaron with Thomas Hibberd, later of Hibberd and Darrin. In 1925, Dietrich moved to Detroit and set up his own company with financial help from the Murray Corporation, a conglomerate of small independent coach-builders, which he had joined upon the advice of Edsel Ford. Soon Packard became one of Dietrich's better customers, so much so that by the time Dietrich decided to leave the security of the Murray umbrella in 1930, most standard production Packard convertibles bore unmistakable signs of his influence.

By 1933, earlier Dietrich designs became the standard production line Packard convertible. Nobody asked Dietrich if this was all right; Packard went ahead and used them anyway. Later, Dietrich would say: "If they stole my name, I was very happy. The publicity didn't hurt!" Dietrich still built custom bodies for the senior Packards, such as the Convertible Victoria. Powered by Packard's smooth V12 engine, the two-door convertible is as perfect as one can get. From the classic grille, along the huge hood, over the split windshield, and on to the trunk, the Packard is pure grace without a line out of proportion. The car is a work of art, pure and simple. This $5,000 Packard wasn't cheap in 1933, but compared favorably with the best Cadillac convertible. Only Duesenberg was far out in the stratosphere, at prices approaching $15,000, and certainly the Packard was every bit its equal in terms of quality, if not speed. There's little doubt that Duesenberg's engine was much faster, and accelerated better; after all, its heritage was motor racing! Still, who would care? Apparently only two or three Dietrich Packard Convertible Victorias were built in 1933. It is a truly unique automobile and the quintessential escapist's dream; smooth as silk, the car's engine purring like a contented cat, the open road invites us for a journey over the hills and far away.

Packard wasn't the only one with fine convertibles in 1933. There was Duesenberg with about 125 units built by Walter M. Murphy of

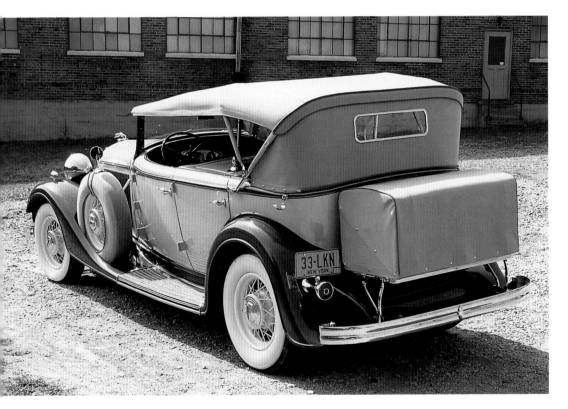

ABOVE RIGHT: *As can be seen by the wood and steel top supports, this 1933 Lincoln KA Dual-Cowl Phaeton is not a true convertible. There is absolutely no place for wind-up windows in this design.*

ABOVE: *Forward hinged doors distinguished the 136-inch (2,229cm) wheelbase Lincoln Model KA from the 145-inch (368cm) model KB. Multi-cylinder engines were all the rage by 1933, the first year that Lincoln adopted a V-12. The 381.7-cubic inch (2,462.6 cubic cm) engine developed 125 bhp in the KA and 150 bhp in the larger KB.*

Pasadena, California who was responsible for fifty-five convertible coupés, all but a handful built on the shorter 142-inch (360.6cm) wheelbase. Convertibles on the 153-inch wheelbase (388.6cm) chassis are rare. About twenty-five convertible sedans were built by Murphy, as well as a few convertible berlines (berline models feature a wind-down center division). Most Murphy-bodied Duesenberg convertibles appeared in 1929 and 1930, and the high-waisted style, probably designed by Franklin Hershey, became the benchmark. The beautiful Murphy boat-tail speedster was the work of Franklin Hershey, and can be seen at the Auburn-Cord-Duesenberg Museum in Auburn, Indiana. It was probably the first speedster to be built on the "J" chassis. Murphy's high-waisted, narrow-window convertible design heavily influenced other coach-builders, such as Bohman & Schwartz and Rollston, who continued the art deco approach throughout their lines.

It was Harley Earl's new V16 Cadillac that broke away from the square, boxy style considered the norm, and introduced a rounded, more streamlined approach. Earl introduced the style in 1932, honing it and refining it for 1933. Full wheel openings characterized the softly rounded fenders, and the long hood featured a curved grille opening that centered into a "V." The bumper adopted four thin chromium bars that wrapped into the fenders. Contrary to the narrow-window theme of Duesenberg, Earl adopted a larger glass area and lower belt line. Even if they were not that popular, most manufacturers offered convertible sedans for those who wanted to treat friends or family to the joys of open-air motoring. Nash came along with the Model 981 convertible sedan complete with landau irons and "Twin Ignition." That meant the in-line-eight engine had two spark plugs per cylinder and developed 94 base horsepower. When it came to styling, however, General Motors was leaving everyone else in the dust with Earl's rounded designs, which took another jump forward in 1934 with semipontoon front fenders on some Cadillacs, backward-sloping grilles and windshields on all GM makes, and the provision of teardrop or pear-shaped headlights across the board. All types of convertibles were offered: convertible coupés, convertible sedans, convertible phaetons, and convertible landaus. (We mustn't forget convertible coupés with a drafty rumble seat where the trunk should be.)

As for the LaSalle, it was a complete departure from the cars of a year earlier. A narrow, slanting upright grille, bullet headlamps, and pontoon-style fenders distinguished the LaSalle from any other GM marque. More than any other, the LaSalle was considered Earl's own—remember, he designed the first—and it was because of Earl that the LaSalle was saved from oblivion after a horrendous 1933. Instead, it became something of a showpiece for the way GM's design was heading. In convertible form the LaSalle was very handsome. There was nothing out of place—the smooth design looked as though it was meant to be a convertible. In fact, the design had its beginnings on the drawing boards of Julio Andrade and Jules Agramonte. Andrade, incidentally, became head of the Cadillac-LaSalle design studio soon after arriving at Earl's studio in 1929. Earl obviously approved Andrade's design and probably helped develop it from the drawings and scale models the team presented to him. Later on, Earl

Here is an example of Art Deco at its best. The plate claims that the 1936 Auburn Boat-tail Speedster had been driven at 100 mph (160kph) and was signed by test driving ace, Ab Jenkins, which was true. Jenkins had driven an Auburn at 100 mph and broke several records at Bonneville Salt Flats in 1935, but the wording suggested he had driven each and every one at that speed.

would suggest themes to his designers, who would interpret them in metal and clay before final approval. So revolutionary was the LaSalle's design that it would set the styling trend for the next few years.

If the LaSalle was a design breakthrough, there were others as well. Pierce-Arrow launched the very advanced, aerodynamic Silver Arrow, of which only five were made. Each sample cost $10,000, and there was no convertible model. At least there was the spectacular 1933 Pierce-Arrow convertible sedan. Powered by a seven-liter (26.4g) V12, the Pierce was a powerful statement for purity in automotive design. Even more revolutionary was the 1934 Chrysler Airflow. Chrysler engineers Fred Zeder, Carl Breer, and Owen Skelton were responsible for the wind-tunnel-tested, aerodynamic car. The Airflow was like a Jell-O mold, very round and very pregnant. The grille was flush with the hood, very curved. There wasn't an upright anywhere, and the car introduced a series of advances, such as putting the rear seat ahead of the axle and the engine over the front axle. To this day, these features are common to any car made anywhere. Americans did not like the Airflow, and Chrysler almost lost its shirt on it. There were no convertible Airflows because the design precluded that, but it is worth mentioning in context with the times. The peak of the Depression had passed and there was noticeable improvement blowing in with the wind. And whatever the Airflow might have been, it exerted a tremendous influence on the industry for years to come.

The powerful hood and grille shape of the Gordon Buehrig-designed Auburn 851 Boat-tail Speedster features front fenders that curve into the body, like wings poised for flight.

Of immediate importance was GM's new all-steel roof, called the "Turret Top" for want of a better description. Naturally, all-steel roofs and bodies added to strength and durability; termites in the Great Plains would have a hard time munching through steel! Chrysler's Imperial model had no convertibles in 1934, possibly because a 1933 total of 375 units sold didn't warrant the expense of building any more. Convertibles have always represented

a small percentage of the overall sales picture, but are more important as a showroom draw. Actually, 375 units out of a 3,989 total wasn't too bad and was certainly better than the Chrysler Royal Eight series. In 1933, 10,389 Royal Eights were built, of which only 796 were convertibles.

TOP: *Art Deco was all the fashion by 1934, as can be seen by the LaSalle's attractive hood ornament. Chrysler went the whole Art Deco route with their advanced Airflow models. Unfortunately, they were too radical to generate public acceptance.*

ABOVE: *Oldsmobile shared its straight-eight engine with LaSalle. In LaSalle's case the engine developed 95 bhp, 5 horsepower more than the Oldsmobile version.*

RIGHT: *Attractive, modern styling of the 1934 LaSalle Series 350 Convertible Coupé was the work of Jules Agramonte, under design chief Harley Earl's direction. Pontoon fenders and a high waistline were Earl trademarks. Note the innovative porthole hood vents, five on each side, that would eventually show up on post-war Buicks.*

With the general public turning away from the fabulous Airflow in droves, Chrysler hastened to build conventional automobiles to complement the car nobody understood and, at the same time, prevent the company from going under. There were a convertible sedan and a convertible coupé in the new 1935 Imperial Airstream 8 Series CZ. The new cars had a lot of the Airflow in their design, plus a fair amount of GM styling, which was turning up on most American marques in one way or another.

Auburn, one of the shining lights in the auto industry, took a turn for the worse after a record 29,536 cars sold in 1931. By 1934, sales had slipped to a desultory 5,536 units. Pulling out all the stops, Auburn had completely new designs done by Gordon Buehrig in 1935, including the legendary 851 Boat-Tail Speedster. The short-lived V12 didn't reappear after 1934; the Depression wasn't the best time to sell multicylinder automobiles. Unfortunately for the Cord triumvirate, nobody was interested in the new 851 series, which included a swish convertible and cabriolet. Studebaker had six convertibles spread across three main series broken up into numerous subseries in 1934. Although sales were up from 1933, demand for the convertibles was so poor that the great South Bend company dropped them all for 1936. The disposal of its convertible lines was mainly due to economic woes; the Depression had taken its toll and, if Studebaker was to survive, something had to give. With the exception of an impressive convertible sedan built in the Commander and President series through 1938–39, there would be no more Studebaker convertibles until 1947.

One of the most stunning convertibles ever to see the light of day was the 1935 Cord 851. Cord's empire was in deep trouble with no salvation in sight. That the new Cord came out was nothing short of a miracle. In late 1933, Cord was in a mess, primarily because of the Depression. His overstretched company was not programmed to suffer major financial losses, such as an 80 percent drop in Auburn sales, and virtually no sales for the Duesenberg. Al Leamy hastily designed a new six-cylinder Auburn for 1934 and work began on the "Baby Duesenberg," to be designed by Gordon Buehrig. The idea was to make a cut-rate luxury car aimed at a more popular market level. Unfortunately, Leamy's 1934 Auburn met with unsympathetic public response, and Buehrig was pulled off the Duesenberg project to try and restyle Auburn for 1935. This he did with wonderful results. First, there was the classic Auburn 851 Supercharged Speedster, then an entire line of heavily face-lifted family cars, including an Auburn 851 Salon Dual Ratio Phaeton. For a car costing little more than $1,400, the Phaeton was, as the prestigious magazine *Special Interest Autos* called it, a "classy classic." It had the dignity and elegance associated with convertibles costing thousands more. It had body-on-frame construction of welded steel, was 199 inches (505.4cm) long, and was powered by Lycoming's new straight-eight putting out 115 base horsepower; supercharged versions claimed 150 horsepower.

In those days, a phaeton's top wasn't the easiest thing to fold down. It is not a matter of unhooking at the front and folding back. It is a serious business requiring two persons' labor. First, the wing nuts tightening the center posts have to be loosened, the center posts carefully removed, and the hinge levers folded back, up, down, up, down, every which way. Patience is required; there are no shortcuts. Try one and *craacck! crunch!* One important hinge bracket broken. Once all these procedures are completed, the top can be lifted and folded back. Of course, phaetons are not made today, and the last four-door convertible was the 1967 Lincoln Continental, which had an electric top. The spoiled motorist of today has only to push a button to let the sun shine in.

Still, the Auburn Convertible Phaeton was a refined car with many advanced features, including the dual ratio gearbox. Returning to the "Baby Duesenberg," the idea was dropped in favor of making the car a new Cord. Money was extremely tight to get on with the job of making the Cord a reality. Sometimes money would be earned by manufacturing and selling kitchen cabinets to Montgomery Ward. (Cord's plethora of shaky companies could turn their hands to anything, it seems.) Like the L-29, the new Cord was to be front-wheel drive. Naturally, the system would not be the same as in the ill-fated original Cord, but a much more advanced unit altogether. As far as looks went, the Cord was destined to be one of the greatest automobile designs ever.

Suddenly, Buehrig and the engineers heard the new Cord was scheduled for the New York Auto Show on November 2, 1935. Buehrig said years later that since the project had restarted, they had only had three months and twenty-six days to build and test a prototype, complete tool-

Fleet and fast is the impression conveyed by Gordon Buehrig's classic design of the 1935–36 Auburn Boat-tail Speedster. Equipped with supercharged power, the car would probably race to 100 mph (160 kph) given the right conditions. Though an open car, the Speedster was not a convertible in the strictest sense: it had no roll up windows.

Gordon Buehrig was asked to face-lift Auburn's entire line for 1935–36, and the 852 Supercharged Convertible Phaeton is one of the beautiful results. Note what are called "suicide doors." Opening the opposite way to each other, the doors could have serious problems, including structural weakness at the center pillar.

ing, and produce finished cars for the show. By some miracle, the impossible was made, well, almost possible. All the cars had to be built by hand for the show, and were completed just in time. Nobody would have guessed from the salesmen's smiles that the Cords wouldn't run because none of them had the new electro-vacuum transmissions, which were not ready in time. To further compound Cord's troubles, no two cars were identical. Never mind the problems, the frustrations, and the lack of money, the Cord 810 was the most beautiful car at the show. It dazzled, it charmed, it delighted. It caused a sensation because it was sensational. With its square, coffin-nose hood, wraparound grille, pontoon fenders, clean, unadorned lines, and its very advanced engineering, the Cord quite literally took the viewer's breath away. In the 810 Sportsman Convertible form, the Cord was just as dazzling, the crème de la crème of cars.

Unfortunately, Cord's troubles were far from over. People placed orders for Cords, many dreaming of moonlit cruises with the top down come next summer. They waited eagerly for the car to arrive at the local dealership. None came. There was always an excuse. To allay frayed tempers, Cord gave customers a miniature brass model. Finally, production

began on February 15, 1936. Many people lost patience after waiting so long, canceled their orders, and bought Buicks or DeSotos instead. Those patient enough to wait were met by a myriad of problems. The gears wouldn't shift, constant velocity joints squeaked and rattled, and the engines overheated. This was not at all what people expected. Rumors spread: the car was no good. A summertime moonlit cruise in the gorgeous convertible was just not the same in a car with noisy constant velocity joints.

Most of the flaws were eventually corrected, but the public relations damage was done. Nobody wanted the beauty with the beast lurking beneath the body contours. By now, rumors were spreading of Cord's downfall, and even if the cars were trouble-free by 1937, nobody wanted to be saddled with a dead duck. Gordon Buehrig said if Cord had not had the six-month delay, the bugs would have been ironed out, and production cars would have been ready for immediate delivery at show time. Instead, after a mere three thousand models were produced from 1935 to 1937, a great American automobile died. Not long after, the 1935–37 Cord was recognized by New York's Metropolitan Museum of Art as a work of art, thus elevating Gordon Buehrig to the position of a sculptor in steel. Or, as

Buehrig would have it: Rolling Sculpture. All creative car designers can rightfully claim to be artists: they create pleasurable, practical art, in steel, like the 810 or 812 Cord Sportsman convertibles.

But there were others, too, such as the 1936 Hudson Eight Convertible. Though following the more conventional lines then in vogue, the Hudson took them a step further. Tall, rounded, wire-mesh-style, die-cast grilles were complemented by a chrome waterfall in the center. Or perhaps a fencer's mask might be a better description. Closed spare wheels adorned the well-rounded front fenders; at the rear, skirts hid the rear wheels, a feature borrowed from the ill-fated Chrysler Airflow.

In 1936, after a one-year hiatus, Chevrolet brought back its convertible cabriolet using the new A-body introduced in 1935. A narrower grille graced the Chevrolet, which was little different from the year before. Pontiac, which adopted Franklin Hershey's chrome Silver Streak hood and grille trim in 1935, toned it down a little for 1936. The Silver Streak would be a Pontiac trademark for the next twenty-one years. Chevrolet and Pontiac shared the A-body and, apart from grilles and interior trim, there was little difference between the two. Product standardization is nothing new, it seems.

In 1933, there were thirty different convertible designs; by 1936, the number had dropped to eighteen, probably due to low sales during the Depression, which, thanks to President Roosevelt's New Deal program, was beginning to recede. Of Ford's eighteen models, there were four convertibles, including a four-door convertible sedan and a two-door club cabriolet. Only one roadster made the lineup; it was a disappearing breed that became extinct by 1938. There was only one engine for all the Fords and that was the famous side valve V8, a favorite unit much coveted by

hot-rodders. A convertible sedan cost $760, the convertible two-door cabriolet $675. Chevrolet's six-cylinder two-door convertible cabriolet was priced at $595. So for $90 more one could have a zippy V8, normally the preserve of much higher-priced cars. Despite the advantage of a V8 that made Ford the overall winner of the Monte Carlo Rally in 1936, it lost the No. 1 spot to Chevrolet by quite a large margin (748,554 to 975,238). A new transcontinental speed record was set by Bob McKenzie driving a standard Chevrolet. Not a convertible, note. With the top up, wind would billow under it, thereby slowing down the car. Also, nobody drives convertibles in NASCAR races because of safety concerns. That's the disadvantage of convertibles; any accident can be very serious for driver and passengers.

As the Depression drifted away, the auto industry counted its losses. By 1937, many great names had fallen by the wayside. Auburn, Cord, and Duesenberg, a trio of wonderfully innovative car-makers, were gone. So were Marmon, Reo, Franklin, Peerless, Mercer, and Stutz. All died between 1930 and 1937. Pierce-Arrow would hang on only until 1938. Competition from the powerful Big Three and the stronger independents helped give the coup de grace to cars that died prematurely. Lincoln, like all other expensive makes, suffered quite a lot during the Depression. To ensure that Lincoln wouldn't follow the other illustrious but unfortunate makes, it was decided that hard times warranted a medium-priced car. So the Lincoln Zephyr was born.

Shown at the end of 1934, the John Tjaarda–designed Lincoln Zephyr was obviously influenced by the Chrysler Airflow's aerodynamic shape, but was a far better-looking car. Power came from Lincoln's 110-horsepower L-head V12. Reaction to the prototype was encouraging. Edsel Ford, a man of elegant taste, loved it. The car was slated for production in 1936, first as a two- and four-door sedan. Nearly fifteen thousand units sold in 1936, which helped Lincoln's coffers no end. Buoyed by this, the original two-door sedan was dropped and replaced by a two-door coupé sedan and a two-door coupé in 1937. A Town Limousine was also added, but no convertibles. That was the big Lincoln K's territory. Under the hood Lincoln used the same V12 engine, but horsepower was 150, compared to the Zephyr's 110. All Lincoln convertible models were supplied by outside coach-builders; there were only four standard body styles and seventeen coach-built models, including four convertibles.

Two convertible sedans were by LeBaron, which also built a convertible roadster. Brunn provided a convertible victoria. Prices ranged from $5,450 to $5,650. Compared to GM's striking convertible models of the same year, the coach-built Lincolns appeared behind the times. There were 877 Lincoln K units sold in 1937, of which seventy-seven were convertibles. This compares with the stylish unit-construction Zephyr, which sold 29,997, double the number for the previous year. In 1938, K models began to catch up with the opposition, following the rounded good looks pioneered by Earl's studio for GM. As for the Zephyr, at last the model was given a convertible for the 1939 season. It was 210 inches (533.4cm) long and it was beautiful, the ultimate expression of Tjaarda's original exquisite design.

Gordon Buehrig's inspired 1936 Cord 810 is recognized as a work of automotive art. This model is a convertible Phaeton. Powered by a 115 hp V-8, the front-wheel-drive Cord was as advanced as it was beautiful, once its initial troubles were ironed out.

Every line of the 1936–37 Cord was—and is—pleasing to the eye. Unfortunately, it did not sell as well as it should have due to production problems and public awareness that the Cord empire was in deep trouble. Nobody wants a car from a company that has gone bust! On the other hand, had people bought the Cord, it might still be with us today.

Of the few independents left, Packard, Studebaker, and Hudson were the strongest. Nash dropped convertibles in 1935, but returned with an interesting cabriolet in 1937. The next season Nash offered a nice but undistinguished Ambassador Six, which didn't quite catch the magic of the 1930–32 Ambassador or the Twin Ignition Eight convertible models. GM built its last roadster and phaeton in 1933, thus leaving the convertible, then six years old, as the only open car in the manufacturer's five-division lineup. By 1936, GM's lead in car-body design was very apparent, and continued uninterrupted until the mid-1950s. As 1936 turned into 1937, America began to see the beginning of the end to the Depression, which actually left GM stronger than ever.

Alfred Sloan became chairman of the company that boasted an attractive, all-new LaSalle convertible sedan priced at $1,680. Oldsmobile, after a huge plant expansion program in 1936, fielded brand-new cars for 1937. Everything about them was new, including a switch from ladder-type frames to a more efficient, lighter crossmember in common with other GM lines. There's little doubt that the best-looking convertibles to come out of GM in 1937 had to be Buick and Cadillac. Eight-cylinder Pontiac and Oldsmobile L-37 convertibles used longer wheelbases than the six-

cylinder models and were also quite handsome. For some reason, the Olds F-37 six-cylinder convertible was very awkward, especially in the grille area. Made up of eight widely spaced, curved horizontal bars, the grille looked as though it didn't belong. As for Pontiac's six-cylinder convertible sedan, it looked clumsy compared to the eight-cylinder cars.

Mention has to be made of the groundbreaking 1936 Buick Century convertible. Harlow Curtice took over as Buick's chief, called the engineers together, and said he wanted a change from the conservative route the division had embarked upon at the beginning of the Depression. Curtice was too late to do anything about the 1934–35 models, but he made sure the 1936 cars reflected his thinking. Pre-Curtice Buicks were known by numbers: Series 40, Series 50, and so on. Curtice kept the numbers, but added names as well. In 1936, the low-priced Series 40 became the Series 40 Special. There was no series 50, but the Series 60 was christened the Century. Then came the Series 80 Roadmaster and the Series 90 Limited. All names meant something. The Roadmaster was the luxury car, the Century the 100-mph (160kph) "supercar"—due to its lightweight body and large, new overhead valve (OHV), 120-horsepower straight-eight. In convertible form, the Century was a very attractive car. It weighed 3,775 pounds (1,713.8kg) and was also reasonably priced at $1,135. The 1936 convertible production was 1,135, not a lot perhaps, but better than others.

A very appealing offering from Chrysler in 1936 was the Airstream C-8 Convertible Coupé. It sat on a 121-inch (307.3cm) wheelbase and was driven by the L-head straight-eight of 273.8 cubic inches (4,486.7 cubic cm), developing 105 horses. The main crossmember frame was strengthened with a sixteen-pound (7.2kg) tubular oval member that encircled the frame, doubling the car's torsional stiffness. A nice detail was the driveshaft passing through the crossmember, with the result that the floor was completely flat in the open-bodied Chryslers. Elements of the misunderstood Airflow were embodied in the Airstream, with the enclosed rear wheel arches being an immediate giveaway. If ever two opposing cars were alike, the honor goes to the 1936 Chrysler Airstream and Buick Century convertibles. Whether they were alike by accident or design is not clear. Certainly, the grilles are very similar, both have rumble seats, and the hood flutes are almost identical. The Century has twin side-mounted spares, while the Airstream mounts one spare beneath the rumble seat. Some say the Chrysler, with its "Floating Power" rubber-mounted engine, had the smoothest ride, but this is a matter for conjecture. Similarities between makes in the same company were becoming more common, thanks to the use of two bodies, and were fairly advanced by the mid-thirties. Pontiac and the Buick Special used the Chevrolet body, but the front, from the windshield forward, was all Pontiac or all Buick. Even the fenders were different. But the 1937 Chevy body was awkward, even in convertible form, with an odd slash that came down the side of the lower hood area, behind the rather small fenders, and into the door. The trunk looked like an add-on and the hood line didn't appear to match the body. Perhaps this was why Harry J. Klingler, Pontiac's general manager, dropped Chevrolet's A-body and switched Pontiac over to the B-body used by Buick and Oldsmobile.

Although it wasn't the greatest design, at least the larger-wheelbase Pontiac convertible sedan could stand on its own merits. Like its smaller brother, the larger Pontiac was all-steel for the first time. Of course, Hershey's famous Silver Streak of ribbed chrome graced the hood, complementing the four chrome grille top bars that extended all the way to the windshield. The rest of the grille, which was standard size, curved to meet the Silver Streak head-on in the middle. An unusual feature of the Pontiac convertible sedan was the placement of the twin sun visors. They were attached to the front top bow of the convertible roof—making them impossible to use with the top down.

Chrysler's 1937 Royal made its first appearance in 1936 as a six-cylinder car designed to appeal to a younger market. The convertible sedan was an interesting model. It sat on a 116-inch (294.6cm) wheelbase with an overall length of 193 inches (490.2cm). As with the Airstream, there was no mistaking the Airflow influence in the Royal. There were the styled fender skirts with the telltale winged emblem, and the grille was the same as the '37 Airflow, featuring the awkward hood side trim blending with the wraparound grille that jutted forward a little too much. Sun visors were positioned on the window frame where they should be, but the head-

lamps sat too high for decent proportioning. Only 177 examples of this particular Royal model were made, which makes it an extremely rare collector's convertible today. To strengthen the car, there is an extra underfloor frame to stiffen the open car's structure, thus resulting in a four-inch-higher (10.1cm) floor over the standard sedans. Still, the car does have a youthful look about it, though it is doubtful very many youngsters ever owned one, let alone sat in one. As always, the luxury cars still left—Packard, Cadillac, Lincoln, Chrysler Imperial, and a very weak Pierce-Arrow—were not ashamed to be seen as the transportation of the very wealthy.

Admittedly, Packard had an attack of goose bumps during the early part of the Depression and came out with a line of cheaper cars in the new 120 series. The 120 certainly helped pull Packard through the bad years, and nobody can say the 1936 120 convertible wasn't a handsome car. It came with a rumble seat, carried the cormorant proudly at its bow, and the finish had the traditional Packard stamp of quality. The convertible started at only $1,110. Even if the junior Packards saved the company for a couple more decades—an even cheaper model, the 110, came in 1937—they helped lose its overall prestige as the car to have. The snooty and the Rockefeller types didn't care to see the gardener driving along in a car with the same grille as theirs, so the rich and the famous started buying Cadillacs. By the end of the thirties, Cadillac was the number one luxury car in the nation.

Into an atmosphere of political uncertainty on one hand and escapism on the other, came a beautiful, new sixteen-cylinder Cadillac convertible. This was the Series 90 convertible sedan. Under the hood was a brand-new V16 engine that, according to the critics, was better than the previous unit. No longer an overhead valve design, the new motor reverted to side valves, and, as there were fewer parts, it was less expensive to make than the overhead valve unit. The OHV 12-cylinder engine was axed, never to return. "Trust the instinct which impels you to choose from the Royal Family of Motordom," read the copy for a 1936 Cadillac advertisement obviously meant to encourage the lordly to switch from Packard to GM's Standard of the World. Actually, the ad would have been far more appropriate in 1938, when the Cadillac Series 90 convertible sedan became the Cadillac to end all Cadillacs. Harley Earl had little to do with it; the car was designed by his successor, Bill Mitchell.

Unlike Earl, who preferred rounded, fleshy lines, Mitchell favored sharp edges. "I don't like dumpy, boxy things," he once said, and he didn't like Harley Earl's designs either. Mitchell probably liked the sensational Buick Y-Job, a long, low two-passenger convertible roadster with many intriguing innovations. Most of the design was done by George Snyder, who worked in the art and color studio under Earl. Recognized as Detroit's first "Show Car," the Y-Job accurately predicted Buick's 1942 styling. Earl was so pleased with the Y-Job that he used it as his car for some time.

Having joined GM in 1935 to work with Earl, Mitchell got the chance to show his ability when he was given the job of designing the 1938 Cadillac Series 60 Special and the Series 90. Mitchell liked the great European classics, and their influence was evident in the two Cadillacs. Mitchell wanted his designs to look powerful and fast, and he achieved this in no small measure. Although only thirteen copies of the $6,000 V16 Series 90 convertible sedan were built, the less expensive, smaller, lighter Series 60 Special managed 315 convertible coupés and sedans. It was a masterful blend of American and European ideas in one cohesive whole. Now regarded as one of the greatest Cadillac designs of all, the 60 Special fulfilled Mitchell's desire for a car that looked powerful, yet was incredibly elegant. In convertible form it ran rings around the opposition.

There really was nothing to touch it, not even the attractive Lincoln Zephyr, which gave birth to its first convertible in 1938. One thousand sixty-one convertibles, in sedan and coupé form, were built that year, which was more than three times the 60 Special output. Driven by Ford's troublesome V12 (it chucked oil every which way but the right one), the Zephyr carved itself a niche because it was inexpensive and possessed an advanced design. And even if the V12 gave cause for worry, buyers overlooked the problems for the panache the car afforded. Pierce-Arrow built only forty cars in 1938, a total made up of eight- and twelve-cylinder models which were carryovers from the year before. It is hardly likely there were any convertibles among them, for Pierce went to the wall early in the year.

Packard, on the other hand, found renewed strength with its mass production 110 and 120 models, but continued making luxurious, high-dollar automobiles, such as the twelve-cylinder dual cowl phaeton by coach-builder Rollston. Custom-made automobiles had become an endangered species by 1938, and were all gone by the start of World War II. Nevertheless, this particular Packard was the cream of the crop, a beauty, the type of car Packard should always have built. The cheapest Packard open car was the 110 Convertible coupé, costing $1,235. If people only knew it, that was a lot of car for the money, rivaling lesser Buicks, Oldsmobiles, and LaSalles. Ford had no medium-priced car (the Zephyr was creeping into the luxury class), but the situation would change the following year. Naturally, Packard, Cadillac, and Lincoln were the top-dollar cars; a Packard Touring Cabriolet by Brunn was the most expensive car in 1938, priced at $8,510.

Of course, there were lots of inexpensive convertibles as well. Dodge had coupé and sedan versions costing the same as Packard's 110, but for $850, there was the smart Plymouth P6, driven by Chrysler's reliable side

valve, 82-horse six. Nineteen-thirty-eight was regarded as a mini-recession year by the industry, with sales falling on all fronts. Plymouth alone dropped from a 1937 high of 514,061 units to 297,572 in '38. A total restyling in 1939 and a healthier economic climate increased sales to more than 350,000, but Plymouth's best was still to come. Everybody had jumped on the Rubenesque bandwagon by 1938, copying the rounded, fleshy designs pioneered by Harley Earl.

Ford had an interesting convertible with headlamps flared into wider-than-usual front fenders. There were two V8 engines offered in either 136- or 221-cubic-inch (2,228.6 or 3,621.5 cubic cm) form. For the second time, Ford thumped the Europeans by winning the classic Monte Carlo Rally. New styling—or should we say major face-lifts—greeted customers in Ford, Chevrolet, and Plymouth showrooms in 1939. A sharply V-ed grille made up of horizontal bars, teardrop headlights mounted flush into the fenders, and optional rear fender skirts gave the Ford convertible coupé a look of motion.

Plymouth followed Ford with a V-shaped front and its version of the horizontal V grille, flanked on either side by horizontal grilles mounted into the splash aprons between fenders and prow. The same theme was adopted by Chevrolet—a V-ed grille flanked by horizontal bars on the splash aprons. Chevys were easily distinguished on a dark night by free-standing headlamps mounted atop the aprons. Both Plymouth and Ford flared theirs into the fenders. For the first time in ages, Plymouth offered both convertible coupés and convertible sedans in 1939. Styled by ex-coach-builder Raymond Dietrich, designer of many legendary cars, the Plymouth was far better looking than the rather stodgy 1938 model.

One thing Ford didn't have, but needed badly, was a medium-priced car to take on Buick, Oldsmobile, DeSoto, Dodge, and Packard. Now that Graham and Hupmobile were ailing and pinning their collective hopes on using revamped 810 Cord body dies, the Big Two, Packard and Hudson, had the mid-priced convertible field all to themselves. Ford wanted a piece of that profitable action. In 1939, Mercury was born. Edsel Ford was personally involved with the conception and styling of the 1939 Mercury, which, at first glance, looked very similar to the Ford. Another look, and differences become apparent. It had horizontal grille bars instead of vertical, its fenders were not so rounded, and it sat on a longer wheelbase. Under the hood was the same V8 as the Ford, but displacing 239.4 cubic inches (3,923 cubic cm). In Mercury guise, the engine pumped out 95 horses, and was quite nippy between the lights. It had standard leather seating instead of cloth, as in the Ford. It was faster, thus earning itself a reputation for being a hot one. Obviously, a lot of people had been waiting for Ford to build a mid-priced car. In its first year, 76,198 Mercurys were produced, putting it into eleventh place overall on the sales charts.

A new look was offered by Nash for 1939, and included three five-passenger cabriolets under the Lafayette, Ambassador Six, and Ambassador Eight nameplates. The cars were more attractive than in 1938, featuring flush-mounted headlights in the fenders and a sharper, narrower grille flanked by mini-grilles in the splash aprons. The new cars were far better looking than 1938 models and an increase in sales of almost twenty-four thousand units showed that the public thought so, too.

Hudson made attractive cars during most of the thirties but the 1937 DeLuxe Eight convertible coupé was particularly striking. For the number of cars sold, Hudson had a huge inventory of models. In 1939, they launched two more series: the 118-inch-wheelbase (299.7cm) Pacemaker and the 122-inch (309.8cm) Country Club series. Of real interest was the Country Club Eight convertible brougham: flush headlights, V-ed grille (not so pronounced as others, but V-ed nonetheless), and twin side mounts. A Terraplane eight-cylinder 254-cubic-inch (4,162.2 cubic cm) L-8 was under the hood. Prices for the brougham competed with the new Mercury, Buick, and DeSoto.

For some curious reason, Chrysler had no convertibles in 1939. Nor did Dodge or DeSoto. Plymouth had only a convertible coupé and sedan. Over at GM, it was a case of mild face-lifts across the board. Packard found itself taking a drubbing from the wealthy as they hopped over to Cadillac, but the 110 and 120 models were doing well in the low- to mid-priced market.

Nineteen-thirty-nine was the last year of an incredible decade of riches to rags, a long drawn-out death of many automobile companies and many banks. LaSalle was languishing and, in an effort to boost sales, Cadillac gave it new sheet metal. Running boards were a thing of the past, yet they could be had as an option on the convertible. Big brother Cadillac had an all-new front end, sharper prow, and a V-ed grille flanked by horizontal curved bars in the catwalk areas. There were convertible coupés offered in three series for 1939, and each was very handsome. So was Buick, which adopted a new grille resembling a four-leaf clover cut in half. Enclosed side mounts were offered as an option on the lower-priced Series 40, standard on up-market models. The 1939 model was extremely popular in Britain, where it was regarded as a great value for the money. Pontiac's 1939 DeLuxe Eight convertible coupé was the prettiest yet made by the one-time Oakland Division. A sharp prow was highlighted by the Silver Streak chrome strip flanked on either side by four sets of four horizontal bars that grew smaller as they neared the bumper. The splash aprons were decorated with twin curved grilles made up of narrow vertical bars on each side. In common with almost everything else at the time, the split windshield curved backward at quite an acute angle.

In early September 1939, about the time Britain was declaring war on Germany, America's auto industry launched its 1940 models, which ranked among the best-looking in the past decade. A new car was born and one died. One sign of the times: the convertible sedan was fast becoming a memory. Convertibles never sold in sufficient numbers to be profitable enough to maintain several different body styles, especially in the northern and Midwestern climes, where people wanted to be cocooned during the severe winters. By the mid-forties, the only convertible type to survive would be the two-door model.

Chapter 3

THE TIMES, THEY ARE A-CHANGIN'

In 1940 America's car industry was beginning to show healthy numbers again. Production was up almost 50 percent over 1939, to 3.3 million units. For convertible lovers, who made up a small percentage of the total, the air along country highways still smelled sweet despite the rumblings of World War II. Ever since GM had pioneered the Art & Color Studio, body design had become an increasingly important factor in the production of an automobile. By 1940, you weren't a car producer if you didn't have a design studio, which probably explains why some of the best-looking convertibles were marketed that year, including a couple of entirely new ones.

Henry Ford had put his son Edsel in charge of Lincoln when Ford bought the company in 1922. Under Edsel's leadership, coupled with his clever design abilities (he was a superb stylist, much taken with European design), Lincoln prospered over the years. Collaborating with the talented E.T. "Bob" Gregorie, Ford's answer to Harley Earl, Edsel brought the Lincoln Zephyr to fruition. Later, the Zephyr became the basis for the startling Lincoln Continental, launched in 1940. The Continental was something else. It was first conceived in 1938 following Edsel's latest trip to Europe. Originally, Gregorie and Ford produced the Continental as a one-off for Edsel to use on his annual vacation in Palm Beach. Everyone who saw the car during that winter of 1938–39 wanted one, so the following winter the Continental went into production as Ford's flagship.

So stunning was the design, it became only the second American car to be recognized as a work of art by New York's Metropolitan Museum of Art. The few convertible Continentals left bring a premium in collector circles today. Out of a total of 404 Continentals produced, only fifty-four were convertibles. The Continental convertible left a message of understated elegance and refinement and class. When raised, the convertible top left the rear passengers in complete privacy. In fact, the sides of the top swept round to meet the doors, while the club coupé was quite open by comparison. With the extra strengthening required for the convertible, the

ABOVE: *Art Deco was still in vogue in 1941, as can be witnessed by the stylish dashboard on the 1941 Chrysler Windsor. The gearshift lever was mounted on the steering column; Chrysler first adopted it in 1939.*
PRECEDING PAGES: *By 1941, radiator grilles were spreading across the whole front of the car. A perfect example is this handsome Chrysler Windsor Convertible. Styling was up-to-date, the horizontal grille working well with the integrated headlights and pontoon fenders. The Windsor was Chrysler's cheapest model and used a six-cylinder engine. The slightly more expensive New Yorker had a straight-eight under the hood.*

Continental weighed more than five thousand pounds (2,270kg). With all that bulk, the V12 engine was hard put to offer performance, even a small amount of it. Consequently, comparable Cadillacs and Packards could always leave the Continental eating their exhausts in a traffic light grand prix. Not that Cadillac, Lincoln, or Packard owners would stoop so low; they would regard such activity with snobbish disdain.

Cadillac and Buick presented much the same cars as they had before. Cadillac introduced a new Series 72 to slot in between the Series 60 and Series 75. More important was the new Series 62, complete with convertibles, that succeeded the Series 61. Built on a 129-inch (327.3cm) wheelbase (three inches [7.6cm] longer than the Series 61), the Series 62 would become one of the most popular Cadillacs of all. GM's B-body had gone as far as it could go by 1939, and poor sales of the B-body cars convinced the world's number one auto company to introduce the new Fisher-designed C-body. It went into production at the beginning of 1940 only in coupé and sedan form, serving certain Cadillac, Buick, Pontiac, Oldsmobile, and LaSalle models. Sales of the new C-bodied cars were strong enough to prompt GM to rush a convertible coupé and convertible sedan into production by the spring of that year.

This significant new body ushered in styling that would evolve into the slab-sided shapes of the late forties and early fifties. With the exception of the LaSalle, all GM models had spreading horizontal grilles. Front fenders were becoming part of the noticeably flattening hoods, and trunks were no longer add-ons but integrated with the body. Running boards were fast disappearing, with the few left offered as no-extra-cost options.

LaSalle, the latest designed by Bill Mitchell, was in its last year, pushed out by Buick's offering the same amount of trim and accessories for the same price, especially on the C-bodied Buicks. The similarity of style between the Buick Century convertible and the LaSalle was strong until one viewed the cars from the front. Mitchell admitted he was always awed by the design of the 1934 LaSalle's narrow horizontal grille (it became a trademark) and kept it for the car's last season. Mitchell once recalled having a 1940 LaSalle convertible, the first white one, and he was very fond of it. Driving a car like the LaSalle must have given a lot of pleasure. The top was operated by vacuum but worked perfectly, sliding into a neat well behind the rear seats. Power was supplied by an L-head V8 developing 130 horsepower that moved the car along at a brisk pace. Rear seat passengers were the ones who had their hair blown all over the place, while the front ones were protected by the windshield, although the two-door coupé was probably more cozy.

A salesman and a man of consummate charm, Howard "Dutch" Darrin convinced Packard that his designs should be added to its 1940 lineup. Darrin liked to fly; he liked to sail; he liked to play polo; he liked to dream of finer things. But most of all, Darrin liked to design automobiles. Not just any automobiles—fine automobiles. Darrin worked as a custom coach-builder, with partner Tom Hibbard, in Paris for a number of years before returning to Hollywood to design specials for movie stars. Several of these were custom-built Packards. Three, a convertible victoria (coupé), convertible sedan, and a four-door convertible sedan, were created

Ford designer Bob Gregorie was the man behind the 1940 Lincoln Continental Cabriolet. This beautiful car was the result of detailed discussions between Edsel Ford and Bob Gregorie. Using the V-12 Lincoln Zephyr as a base, Gregorie created the Continental in about an hour. Edsel Ford liked the design so much he asked that it stay exactly as it was; thus, the Continental was born.

loved the rotund theme, which he developed in one form or another until his retirement. ("He liked rounded hoods. I never did. I liked sharper things," said Bill Mitchell, who succeeded Earl at the studio.) The 1940 Chevrolets were fatter than ever and had eschewed the classic radiator grille for eighteen thin, horizontal chrome bars wrapping around the prow and back along the aprons, thus emphasizing the now fashionable wider look. Buick followed with an almost identical grille with fewer, but thicker, bars. An extra-cost, vacuum-operated top was offered for the first time on Chevrolet convertibles, no doubt much to the relief of those stuck with trying to raise their tops manually in sudden rainstorms. Since the beautiful Buick Y-Job show car of 1938, there had been a noticeable shift to horizontal grilles. By 1940, vertical grilles were definitely the exception to the rule. A very attractive example of the old-fashioned vertical grille was the LaSalle and the LaSalle-like Nash Ambassador Eight and Ambassador Six. In fact, their hood prows came to an even finer point than the LaSalle, and the narrow grilles were made up of horizontal bars. On the aprons at either side of the grille, the Ambassador displayed vertical chrome grilles from the nose to the headlights, rather like the cross on a hot-cross bun. The Packard retained its elegant classic grille much in the same way Rolls-Royce and Mercedes have always done.

For 1941, Nash came in with some real changes. Separate body and chassis construction gave way to unit body-chassis assembly. The low-priced Lafayette, with a 117-inch (297.1cm) wheelbase, was cast aside and replaced by the smaller, 112-inch (284.4cm) 600 series. Although there were plenty of coupés, sedans, and even a brougham, the 600 had no convertibles. Both Ambassadors continued with their cabriolet convertibles and had a minor, if somewhat curious, front end face-lift. A thin chrome strip replaced the narrow grille on the pointed "nose," and the horizontal apron bars were modified and moved up to headlamp height. Horizontal bars were placed behind the bumper and extended full width across the front with a break in the middle. Both convertibles had straight six- or eight-cylinder power, the latter engine being the twin-ignition unit of 260.8 cubic inches (4,273.7 cubic cm).

Hudson was believed to have had the strongest, safest convertibles of all in 1941, thanks to its heavily reinforced frame specially designed to

by Darrin on Packard's Super Eight (Series 180) platform. There is little doubt that Packard thought Darrin's custom designs might help it retake its old position as America's premier luxury car. Few debate that the Darrin Packards of 1940 and '41 were among the most beautiful cars built; the convertible sedan was perhaps the most stunning of its genre for many a year. Everybody raved over the convertible coupé, with its rakish lines, acutely slashed door, and its long, low profile. The Darrin Packards were more than cars; they were works of art. And works of art cost money: $4,600 for the two-door and $6,300 for the convertible sedan. Those amounts were more than most were prepared to spend, especially when they could buy a 110 Packard convertible coupé for $1,110. It may not have been as stylish, but at least it was a convertible with a pedigree.

After a successful first year, Mercury came back with only minor changes. The grille was more slanted and the faired-into-the-fender headlamps had more chrome. Compared to the lithe, hungry-looking Darrin Packard, the Mercury convertible coupé was very round, chubby even. Actually, the plump-car look was the responsibility of Harley Earl. He

meet the problems encountered with convertible construction. In any event, convertibles were given little extra support to prevent body flexing or distortion, possibly due to Detroit's ongoing penny-pinching habits to ensure maximum profitability. And there was always the excuse that convertibles realized a very small portion of an automaker's sales. Hudson broke with tradition, which eventually spurred all other makers to follow their lead.

Of the low-priced trio, Plymouth convertibles took a back seat in styling, especially when compared to Chevrolet. Anyone with a sense of class and esthetics put his dollars down on the handsome Chevy two-door Special DeLuxe without even bothering to look at the Ford with its semi-vertical grille and chrome side bars. Chevrolet had replaced vertical grilles in favor of the horizontal theme.

At GM, the vertical grille was also replaced by the new, horizontal grille. Cadillac had a massive appearance accentuated by a broad, horizontal egg-crate grille designed by Arthur Ross, a stylist in the Art & Color Studio. Ross joined the studio in 1936 and will be remembered for Cadillac's trademark grille, which continues to this day in one form or another. Oldsmobile's revolutionary Hydra-Matic automatic transmission, introduced in 1940, became a Cadillac option. LaSalle was replaced by the returning Cadillac 61 series, for which there were no convertibles. Only two were available in 1941 and both were Series 62 models. One was the convertible coupé, the other the by now almost extinct convertible sedan. Buick had a couple of convertible phaetons and Oldsmobile had one. By 1942 they had all disappeared.

Logic tells us the convertible sedan and phaeton were from another place, another time. Convertible coupés were swish, young at heart, and meant for two. People sitting in the back seat of a convertible sedan suf-

RIGHT: *The 1941 Chrysler Windsor's horizontal grille shows the attractive emblem that remained with Chrysler for a number of years. Even though this Windsor had three bumper guards, the bumper itself was not as massive as some.*

BELOW: *The side-valve six-cylinder engine that powered the Windsor had been in production since 1934 and was used in Plymouth, Dodge, and DeSoto models. A very sound engineering design, the engine remained in production through 1958, only being replaced by an overhead valve "Slant Six" in 1959.*

fered the disadvantages of windswept hair, chills, and separation from the conversation up front. As far as privacy went, if romance were in the air, well, there was none back there. Besides, these sedans were more expensive to build. Many were handsome cars, but handsome is as handsome does—and they didn't.

Another fatality was Cadillac's V16 engine. Even the simpler side valve engine was too expensive to continue in anything but mass production. All Cadillacs from 1940 on would rely on V8 power, though there was an exception much later on when Cadillac blotted its copybook with the ghastly Cimarron, powered by a small four-cylinder unit, circa 1982 to 1986. Buick got a bit uppity when it found itself graced by Britain's King Edward VIII, who ordered Buicks for his cars of state during his short reign. GM had to stop Buick's efforts to take over Cadillac's position as

top car. Buick had always prided itself on fine, well-built automobiles loved by many, including the British, who bought large quantities of them. When it came to convertibles, Buick offered some beauties. Buick always promoted convertibles very heavily, with the result that it built and sold more than anyone else. Divided among Buick's three series, 18,569 two-door convertibles were built in 1941. Compare that to Hudson's one thousand in the same year.

Over at Highland Park, Chrysler came out with a slightly face-lifted line of cars. New though, was the Town & Country station wagon with real wood decoration along the sides. With slight trim changes, the already handsome Chrysler New Yorker, Windsor, and Highlander convertible coupés were even more handsome in 1941. Art deco was featured strongly on the dashboard. Chrysler had made a point of featuring art deco motifs

in its designs since 1934. In one of those cases of "letting it all hang out," Chrysler let its designers follow their desires, resulting in the beautiful Thunderbolt convertible show car and the Newport Dual Cowl Phaeton. Six of each open car were built and exhibited across America, bringing traffic—and sales—to Chrysler showrooms.

From the cornfields of Indiana, a state famous for classic cars that went bust, came the Crosley. Developed by radio pioneer Powel Crosley, Jr., the little Crosley survived until 1952. When it first appeared in 1939, it was a diminutive car that succeeded in attracting customers who wanted little runabouts. Power came from an air-cooled Waukesha two-cylinder engine of 35.3 cubic inches (578.4 cubic cm) developing 12 horsepower. Several models were offered, from sedan to tiny station wagon, including, of course, a convertible coupé. It wasn't pretty—it was cute. In convertible form, it was quite sweet, very fast (it could do up to 90 mph [144kph]), very safe, and had excellent handling qualities.

By the time the United States declared war on Japan on December 11, 1941, four days after the infamous attack on Pearl Harbor, 1942 car production was already quite advanced. It continued into February 1942, when the government ordered an immediate shutdown of civilian auto production. Even so, the auto industry had been gearing up for war for some time and was ready to meet the massive arms contracts that would sustain it throughout the hostilities. It is worth mentioning some of the interesting convertibles produced for that truncated season.

Buick and Cadillac displayed the shape of things to come with truly dramatic and advanced styling. An evolution of the 1941 design, the grille's crosshatch pattern had become an egg crate. Long pontoon-shaped fenders extended far into the doors, the rear ones on the 129-inch-long (327.6cm) wheelbase Series 62 convertible—the only Cadillac convertible for the season—blending into the two-door body style. There was no sign of Bill Mitchell here. This had to be Harley Earl, if the sensuous, rounded body and fenders were anything to go by. Buick was all Earl, its styling very close to the Y-Job. Two convertibles were offered in the 124-inch (314.9cm) Series 50 Super and 129-inch (327.6cm) Roadmaster. The front fenders swept all the way back to meet the rear ones, and were emphasized by twin chrome strips extending from behind the front wheel openings to the rear bumper. Bumpers, incidentally, were massive, wraparound affairs that foretold what was to come. Both Cadillac and Buick convertibles were the stuff Hollywood dreams were made of: romance, starlets, the cars to arrive at the Oscars in. A few steps down the ladder, we step into a lower price range. At $1,245, the beefy-looking Dodge Custom convertible coupé had massive bumpers and fender-top high, horizontal grilles meeting the faired-in headlamps; with these features, the Dodge looked as intimidating as an angry bull elephant. Thick chrome streaks were lavished affectionately all over the portly body, but didn't hide the fact that the Dodge was ungainly.

Even cheaper ($1,215) was the equally intimidating Mercury convertible coupé. Masses of chrome on a face-lifted body carried two full-width horizontal grilles. The main one consisted of eight horizontal bars plus hood lip, extending from headlight to headlight. Then a five-bar grille

pushed to each end of the headlights. Choosing an inexpensive convertible would be a toss-up between the popular Plymouth convertible coupé, selling for $1,078, and the Dodge. Both shared the new box perimeter frame, made sturdier for convertible use. Unfortunately, the Plymouth, like the Dodge, was not a beautiful car, but its personality suggested strength and durability. Apparently, this is what most people wanted in their convertibles: 2,806 Plymouth convertibles were produced, compared to Chevrolet's 1,182. Even Dodge beat Chevrolet by three units in the convertible stakes.

The 1942 Ford Continental lacked the graceful elegance of the 1940 convertible, replaced by a flattened hood and unpleasant semihorizontal grille, which was not a styling tour de force. In fact, the front of the Continental had a coffin-nose look that didn't do much for the convertible. On the other hand, Packard retained a vertical grille, which looked more like the old LaSalle's, on its new model, the Clipper, which practically took over Packard, so successful was it in 1941. Designed by Werner Gubitz, the Clipper had flowing fenders disappearing into the door edges, and fully covered pontoon rears. This was a stunning car in convertible form and sold very well.

By the end of February, the entire U.S. auto industry had converted over to war production, and there would be no new cars until 1946. According to *Fortune* magazine, there was a danger that transportation would break down as a result of no new civilian vehicles being built during the war. Thirty million families allegedly owned thirty-two million cars in 1941; by war's end, the number had dropped to twenty-two million as cars broke down, rusted away, or were junked to end up as part of a Sherman tank. Whether *Fortune* was correct, or using scare tactics to drum up business for the auto industry, is not important. Actually, the industry needed no help; everybody, including returning GIs, wanted new cars. Demand was so great it didn't really matter what the car looked like, or how good or bad it was. If it was new, it was sold. Detroit responded quickly to the huge demand for automobiles, rushing out warmed-over 1942 models. A bit of chrome here, a trim change there, and suddenly, a new 1946 model was on the showroom floor. By the end of calendar year 1946, Detroit had built 3.5 million new/old cars.

Changes on all "new" American cars were so few that they are hardly worth mentioning. There were two significant convertible models, one from Ford, the other from Chrysler. Ford offered two convertibles, a DeLuxe and Super DeLuxe, the latter a rather different car, since it used white ash and mahogany panels on doors and trunk. This novel Ford, called the Sportsman, stemmed from sketches made by Bob Gregorie during the war and was an almost unique way of dressing up an old body in a new suit.

Chrysler converted its 1941 Town & Country wood station wagon into a three-model lineup, consisting of six- and eight-cylinder sedans and convertibles, and a hardtop coupé, in 1946. Unlike the new models from Ford and Mercury, which also made its own Sportsman, the Town & Country was more than a dressed-up '42; it had become a highly personalized luxury car. The eight-cylinder convertible was based upon the 127.5-

The unique 1940 Chrysler Newport Dual-Cowl Phaeton was built for the auto show circuit as a public relations exercise. Six Newports were built by LeBaron, and one was chosen to pace the 1941 Indianapolis 500. Millionaire Henry J. Topping bought this particular car, which he modified by installing a Cadillac engine and transmission. He also added his initials to the grille. When he married the film actress Lana Turner, he had the Newport's license plates personalized with her name.

inch (323.8cm) New Yorker, while six-cylinder models shared the 121.5-inch (3086.1cm) Windsor wheelbase. There were no six-cylinder convertibles in the Town & Country line; all Chrysler convertibles used only eight-cylinder engines. The highest price for any 1946 Chrysler was $2,743, but well worth it, considering the exclusivity the Town & Country allowed. It used white ash framing, which helped to add structural rigidity to the doors and decklid. Within the beautifully finished and varnished ash, which was fitted together with interlocking miters, there was a darker, mahogany-veneered plywood. Convertible interiors were finished in top-grade leather, Bedford cord, and wood.

More than anything else at the time, the Town & Country convertible became the car to be seen in and the car to have. Hollywood adored it. Although based on a New Yorker, a T&C convertible had the charisma of an Auburn Boat-Tail, a Duesenberg, a V16 Cadillac. Between 1946 and 1948, 8,380 T&C convertible coupés were produced, figures that put the car into Rolls-Royce territory. Much of the Town & Country was hand-finished, rivaling the Rolls for quality. It became the darling of the rich and famous: Bob Hope, Barbara Stanwyck, Clark Gable, Marie McDonald, Leo Carillo (he played Pancho, the Cisco Kid's sidekick), and

Ray Milland all owned Town & Country convertibles. (Presumably, Leo Carillo liked to be noticed; his T&C had a longhorn's head adorning the hood, and seats covered with the hide of the unfortunate animal.)

Buick and DeSoto had handsome convertibles in 1946 and, while little was changed from 1942, DeSoto went a step further by merging the front fenders into the doors. (Buick did that in 1942 and was the least changed car of all.) Packard had no convertibles in 1946, though Hudson had an attractive Super Six that garnered a little more than one thousand in sales. Apart from one make, nothing would appear until 1948—the year for all new postwar cars. Not that it mattered; 1947 production was way over five million units and among that total was an all-new Studebaker that predated everyone else by a full year.

French-born Raymond Loewy had made a name for himself as an industrial designer extraordinaire; he actually shaped the Coca-Cola bottle, among many other things. He also designed cars, and his studio had been associated with Studebaker since 1938. An important figure in his studio was Virgil Exner, an avant-garde designer if ever there was one. It was Exner who styled the flamboyant "Suddenly it's 1960" Chrysler Corp. automobiles. Exner had a lot to do with the 1947 Studebaker, which was

the first slab-sided car to be put into volume production. Exner based his design on ideas Loewy had developed long before the Studebaker came to fruition. When it was unveiled to the public for the first time, the rest of the auto industry was undoubtedly shaken to the soles of their shoes by a newer-than-new car that had a low profile, only the vestiges of a rear fender, and a lot of glass. Studebaker did well in 1947, producing 139,299 cars, of which 3,300 were convertibles in Champion and Commander models. Of the five body styles, the convertible was the best looking. A shorter-than-usual hood blended well with the longer, swept-down rear, and the car was pleasingly uncluttered, unlike its competition, who used chrome as a way to hide a 1942 body.

On the home front in 1948, car sales continued at a booming pace. Hudson and Packard had sensational new designs, especially Hudson with its roly-poly slab-sided look and revolutionary step-down floor design. Hudson convertibles were known as Brougham convertible coupés and came in three series: Super Six, Commodore, and Commodore Eight. All shared the same wheelbase of 124 inches (314.9cm) and the Super Six had a new six-cylinder engine, the appropriately titled 262-cubic-inch (4,293.3 cubic cm) "Super Six" developing 121 horsepower. This engine was a strong, powerful unit. In the early '50s, it led Hudson to one NASCAR victory after another. Some 117,200 Hudsons were produced in 1948, but only two hundred were convertibles. Of that total, only 64 were eight-cylinder cars. It's surprising so few were built because the unit body and step-down design made for a handsome car indeed.

A Super Eight and a Custom Eight were the two convertibles Packard built on its first truly postwar design. Packard, like Hudson, adopted the flow-through, slab-sided look, but somehow the new Packards didn't look like Packards anymore. "Pregnant Elephant" was the unkind description, referring to the round, rather dowager-duchess shape with massive horizontal bars and a mini-caricature of its former respected grille. Some said Packard was rather like Rip Van Winkle. It had gone to sleep in an older, gentler society, and was unable to adapt successfully to the social upheaval that came after the war. Still, nobody really cared in 1948; a car was a car, so buy it, was the attitude then. Packard had the second-best year in its entire history, with sales of 98,897 units, of which 8,868 were convertibles. They were good convertibles, too. Richly endowed with fine leathers and fabrics, the convertibles were smart cars for those who thought Packard's fine name still meant something. Actually, it was Cadillac that now possessed the top people's-car crown, and in 1948 it was easy to see why: the new design was startling and fit right into the "Brave New World" Aldous Huxley wrote about. There was little doubt it was the car design of the year, eclipsing Hudson and Packard.

The story goes that designers Harley Earl, Bill Mitchell, Franklin Hershey, and Art Ross had been much impressed by the shape of the P.38 Lockheed Lightning fighter airplane they saw just before the war. During the war years, they would doodle ideas for cars incorporating many of the aircraft's salient features, including the twin tail fins. Eventually, many of these ideas found their way onto the 1948 Oldsmobile and Cadillac, the latter having the most dramatic touch of all—the tail fins!

Though not recognized as a classic, the 1948 Cadillac should be. There were 5,450 convertibles of this beautiful car produced, all as Series 62 models. Superb from all angles, the 1948 Cadillac remains one of the postwar era's finest-looking cars, and a heart-stopper as a convertible coupé. It was probably this car that cemented Cadillac's lasting dominance as the luxury car leader. Apart from the Oldsmobile, there were several important new post-war designs, two of them Cadillac and Hudson; the rest waited until 1949. Not that there was any need to change, as the industry could sell everything it produced at that time.

Then the public was thrown into a tizzy; everything was new in the last year of a decade that changed the face of the world. Cadillac was the big, big news over in the GM camp. Not that there was new styling. There wasn't; the car remained faithful to its classic 1948 look. What was new couldn't be seen unless one raised the hood. And there it was: a brand-spanking-new OHV V8 displacing 331 cubic inches (5,424 cubic cm) and developing 160 horses. It weighed two hundred pounds (90.6kg) less than the old side valve engine, could top one hundred mph (160kph) with ease, and was versatile enough to be pushed from a compression ratio of 7.5:1 to 12.1. In a few months, this engine would show its prowess in the competition arena, and very well, too.

K.T. Keller was the head of Chrysler and a man who cared little for style, especially if the result was what he assessed as discomfort in the automobile. Chrysler's 1949 cars reflected his attitude; although they followed the slab shape, they were squarer and higher than the cars from GM or Ford, and one was able—just as Keller wanted—to wear a hat seated behind the steering wheel. It was disappointing, what with the innovative convertibles coming from GM and the independents. Plymouth was just as bad. Solid as a rock but dull as dishwater. Even the new Chrysler Town & Country convertible coupé was a bit of a letdown; it lacked the charisma of the previous model, it had less wood (a material called Dinoc was used between the wood framing), and was too square in shape.

Ford, however, had a wow of a lineup and a gorgeous convertible to boot. Ford had been trailing both GM and Chrysler since 1935, partly due to Henry Ford's insistence on leaving well enough alone. Because of this,

ABOVE: *Harley Earl's 1948 Cadillac design featured the rear pontoon fenders he was so fond of, with the addition of a little tail fin, inspired by the P-38 Lockheed Lightning pursuit fighter he saw at a local airbase. Not only the tail, but the front fenders, curved windshield, and pointed nose were borrowed from the P-38.*

LEFT: *Now you see it, now you don't. Cadillac solved the problem of where to put the fuel filler by tucking it under one of the taillights. To open the taillight, one pressed the button above the horizontal strips.*

Ford lost second place to Chrysler in the mid-thirties. With Henry Ford II and his "whiz kids" heading the company since 1944, Ford became alive and youthful. In 1949, the result of all that corporate youth exploded on the scene with an array of mouthwatering new designs. Of course, Ford regained its number two position with massive sales to a public appreciative of designs that, once and for all, put the thirties, the Depression, and the war behind them. Not even Ford's arch-rival, Chevrolet, could match the Dearborn baby's style.

There was little to touch the 1949 Ford for styling, regardless of price. It took the slab-sided design to its logical conclusion completely flat from stem to stern. Unlike the rounded, Rubenesque look favored by GM, the Ford was square. Its design didn't rely upon acres of chrome to make a statement. As for the convertible (there was only one in the Custom

series), it was the car for the young at heart. From its round, spinnerlike grille center to its bustle-back trunk, the car was a winner. Design credit goes to George Walker, Dick Caleal, and Robert Bourke. Walker was a freelancer, Caleal worked for him, and Bob Bourke was then chief designer at Loewy's studio. Knowing it would need a new car if it was to survive, Ford asked for ideas from freelance studios as well as its own. Walker's team won with its modern body, to which Bourke added the spinner in the grille. A year later, virtually the same spinner popped up on the new Studebaker.

Well over one million Fords were produced in 1949, of which 51,133 were convertibles. The slow-selling Sportsman convertible didn't make it; the only wood look was on the handsome new station wagon. Still, Ford hadn't seen figures like this since 1937; they helped wrest the number two spot away from Chrysler. Don't forget, all these Fords offered the chance of flathead V8 power, which the majority chose over the in-line Six. With 100 horses under the hood, Ford was the low-price leader at the traffic-light grand prix, and its convertible was the darling of the starlets trying to attract attention along the boulevard. In any form, but especially convertible form, the Ford made a statement. It was driving into the Brave New World and beyond.

Not that Ford forgot its other siblings. Both Mercury and Lincoln were given complete redesigns. Ford's chief designer, Bob Gregorie, was responsible for the 1949 Mercury, a car he considered the best work he ever did. Unlike the Ford, which he contemptuously passed off as a "styled by committee car," Gregorie's Mercury was far more rounded and looked fatter than the Ford. In a sense, it looked as though Gregorie and his team had taken a 1948 body, stretched the front fenders to merge into the doors, then hammered the rear ones flat. The trunk was semi-fastback in shape, with the grille looking like a tight wire coil divided at the center by a vertical chrome shape. An enlarged version (255.4 cubic inches [4,185.2 cubic cm]) of Ford's L-head V8 provided power. Mercury's 1949 convertible was a striking automobile costing $2,410. There were 16,765 convertibles built out of a 1949 Mercury total of just over 300,000 units. Mind

George Walker and Bob Gregorie were part of the design team at Ford that created cars such as the 1949 Customline Convertible which propelled Ford into second place between GM and Chrysler.

you, nice as the convertible was, it turned out that the two- and four-door coupés became legend. As every car book on the planet will gladly inform you, James Dean drove a '49 or '50 Merc in the classic movie, *Rebel Without a Cause*, and then there's the huge hot-rod fraternity to whom 1949–51 Mercurys are the classic shape for hotting up, customizing, or low riding. There are, however, some very distinctive, customized Mercury convertibles to be found, though they are very scarce.

Sharing the same body, there wasn't much to choose from between the Mercury and standard Lincoln, except snob appeal and extra length. The Lincoln grille was different and not very appealing, but the engine was larger and more powerful. There was a single two-door convertible priced at $700 more than the Mercury. Another convertible, priced at $1,500 extra, was the new Lincoln Cosmopolitan. The Cosmopolitan replaced the V12 Lincoln Continental that was phased out in 1948. A wheelbase extended by four inches (10.1cm) and seven extra inches (17.7cm) overall told you that this was the top Lincoln. In those days, length was identified with luxury and expense. Differences abounded between the standard Lincoln and the Cosmopolitan. The larger car had a one-piece windshield, the Lincoln a two-piece. Like the Mercury, the Lincoln had front fenders that merged into the doors; the Cosmopolitan had none. There was a distracting hunk of chrome over the front fenders that otherwise spoiled a handsome line devoid of brightwork.

During the war, a number of entrepreneurs became wealthy producing armaments for the war effort, all the while dreaming of building the car to end all cars. Well-known attempts came from Preston Tucker, Henry J. Kaiser, and Joseph W. Frazer. While the Tucker saga reads like a Shakespearean tragedy, Kaiser and Frazer successfully got together with Graham-Paige and obtained a huge Willow Run, Michigan, factory once used by Ford for building bombers. Shortly afterward, Graham-Paige dropped out of the picture, leaving Kaiser and Frazer to build cars under their own names. Along with Studebaker, Kaiser and Frazer were the only all-new models pitching the new slab-side look and a six-cylinder engine derived from Continental and built by K-F. They brought out their first convertible in 1949, probably encouraged by their astonishing sales record in their first two years. In 1947, K-F production began on two pretty conventional cars, designed principally by Howard Darrin. As convertibles, both cars were quite handsome because of Darrin's unique design. Economics forced K-F to use the same four-door sedan body and chassis for the convertible, the latter achieved simply by slicing off the roof and leaving the window frames fixed. It took the engineers a lot of time to convince management that the rest of the industry didn't just slice off roofs; they reinforced the cars with strengthened pillars, and used X-frames for structural integrity necessary for such a car.

It was the end of another decade, a troublesome one that left the world older and wiser. Perhaps the fifties would be better; perhaps the wounds of a generation would heal. One thing was for sure: America was on a roll and Americans were looking to the good life. As for the car industry, the next decade was to be one of beauty and some of the wildest art ever seen on four wheels.

Chapter 4

CRUISIN' WITH THE WHITE TOP DOWN

Revelers the world over welcomed in a bright, promising 1950. With the vestiges of World War II growing smaller in rearview mirrors, there were millions of sensible people doing sensible things, living sensible lives, and buying new cars.

Ford, having wrested the No. 2 spot from Chrysler, left well enough alone. So did GM for the most part, although Buick insisted on making its grille into the ugliest buckteeth ever seen. But otherwise, GM relied on minor trim changes for the most part. Nineteen fifty was a record-breaking production year for the auto giant, which produced a mammoth 3,818,033 cars, trucks, and buses—a million more than in 1949.

At war's end, auto manufacturers wasted no time in returning to car production. Soon the assembly lines were churning out slightly warmed-over 1942 vehicles for a car-starved public who didn't care whether the model was old, as long as the car itself was shiny and new. Studebaker thought otherwise: they rehashed a few, very few, 1942 models, then came out with an all-new car in the spring of 1946. By so doing, Studebaker scooped the rest of the industry by two years. The 1950 Studebaker Champion Regal DeLuxe Convertible shown here has a facelifted 1947 body, and is unusual for its "cyclops" middle section.

Chrysler had all-new styling in 1949, which tended toward practicality rather than fashion. Chrysler chairman K.T. Keller preferred sedate cars, and the new cars certainly lived up to his expectations: they were high, they were square, and, eventually, they nearly ruined Chrysler. Chrysler goofed when it reduced the Town & Country to one convertible model in 1949; only one thousand were produced. For 1950, Chrysler compounded the error by dropping the convertible and introducing a two-door hardtop in its place. That didn't help at all; only seven hundred were built, so in 1950, after a few short years, Chrysler dropped what was one of the best automobiles around.

The Chrysler Plymouth looked more like the Chevy, as it went from square to rounded styling. But the big news at Chrysler was the introduction of a radical new engine design that swept the industry off its wheels, the OHV hemispherical head V8. If Cadillac performed well at the 1950 24 Hours of Le Mans in France, then Chrysler's hemis, under the hoods of millionaire Briggs Cunningham's racers, would do even better at the same annual event. Here was an engine that was complex yet versatile, that could perform in a highway convertible or take on Ferraris and Jaguars on the track. On the styling side, Chrysler also adopted a rounder look in its 1951 face-lift, which in convertible form was quite handsome. If the hemi engine was massaged a little, a New Yorker convertible would blow virtually everything off the street. Displacing 331 cubic inches (5,424 cubic cm), the same as Cadillac, the hemi engine developed a conservative 180 horses.

Buick returned to good sense and good taste by performing orthodontic surgery on its grille. Changing the bucktooth look helped the car's design immeasurably, particularly the convertible, which was better balanced without the ground-scraping teeth. There was a new 1951 Special convertible, giving Buick's least expensive range an open-air car.

Entrepreneur and salesman Earl "Madman" Muntz decided he wanted to join Tucker, Kaiser, Frazer, Cunningham, and other hopefuls by creating and producing the car to end all cars. The result was the Muntz. Early models were built of aluminum; later cars were of steel. Muntz claimed his Muntz Jet would do over 128 mph (206km); it sold for around $5,000–$6,000.

Government restrictions cut back automobile production in 1951, but the industry sold almost everything it could build. Station wagons and the new pillarless hardtops were in huge demand. Plymouth led station wagon production with forty-five thousand units. Apart from minor grille and trim changes, GM cars were hardly altered. Ford, too, relied on much the same designs; the Ford now had two smaller spinners in its grille, Mercury and Lincoln had new grilles and squarer rears.

An interesting, albeit short-lived, car was the Muntz Jet. The brainchild of promoter Earl "Madman" Muntz, a man who sold Model T Fords when he was ten, later operated used-car lots, and then turned to selling car radios, the Muntz automobile first appeared in 1949. Powered by Cadillac V8s in the early stages and Lincoln motors later, the Muntz convertible had slab-sided styling, a wraparound grille-cum-bumper, and supposedly did 128 mph (204.8kph). This unique car lasted until 1954, with 394 units produced.

A total restyling found Packard's pregnant look over, and the carmaker once termed America's Rolls-Royce returned to lithe, slimmer proportions. John Reinhart was the designer behind the much-improved shape, which used 122- and 127-inch (309.8 and 322.5cm) wheelbases. The well-built, luxuriously trimmed 250 convertible, Packard's only open-top offering in 1951, was very attractive. The standard 250 engine was the 327-cubic-inch (5,358.5 cubic cm) L-head straight-eight. The manual transmission version developed 150 braking horsepower (bhp), the automatic had 155. Most convertibles probably had the automatic; changing gears didn't seem quite right in a luxury convertible costing over $4,000.

Both Nash and Hudson fielded convertibles, with the Hudson little changed since 1948. Both companies were doing well, Hudson producing over 131,000 units, though, oddly, convertibles lagged far behind, with only 1,651 units made. As for Nash, there were no convertibles in the full-sized Ambassador and Statesman series, but one in the 100-inch-wheelbase (254cm) Rambler, first introduced in 1950. Shaped a bit like a sponge, the little car was as slab-sided as you could get and had enclosed wheels. But the convertible was cute, an ideal open car for the young and adventurous (because of its unique rollback top, college kids were able to stand upright in the car, hanging onto the thick window frames all round). Priced at $1,993, the little Rambler convertible was a great buy.

ABOVE: *The Muntz interior was quite attractive and sported a pleasing array of round instruments. Note the wide transmission hump in the middle of this specimen.*

RIGHT TOP: *Nash chairman George W. Mason loved small cars. So in 1950, he bucked the "bigger is better" philosophy and introduced the 100-inch (254cm) wheelbase Rambler to his line. The model shown—there were only two—is the Custom Landau Convertible Coupé. The other model was the Custom Station Wagon.*

RIGHT BOTTOM: *While it may not have been the prettiest car around, the little Rambler was very advanced for its day, and had a unique roll-back convertible top. The emblem on this model is an aftermarket attachment.*

The 1951 Frazer Manhattan convertible sedan was an unusual convertible. A product of the Kaiser-Frazer Corporation, founded in July 1945, the Manhattan was powered by a six-cylinder engine adapted from a Continental "Red Seal" industrial unit. Limited funds restricted making the convertible from ground up. Makeshift at best, the engineers merely sliced off the sedan roof and installed a stronger X-frame. All things considered they did a miraculous job, but the company failed in 1955.

In 1952, due to the Korean War, defense took priority, and cars were cut back by government order. GM's volume was only 65 percent (nearly two million fewer) of its 1950 total. Buick fielded convertibles in its three series for the first time in 1952, and the Roadmaster was so luxurious it challenged Cadillac for top honors. Chrysler made few changes of any note, but Ford came out with a brand-new line of sharp-looking cars from all three marques.

Ford had heralded a completely new look in 1949 and was doing it again in 1952. The rounded lines were replaced by a lower and wider square look. Finally, the split windshield gave way to a single curved piece

of glass, but the spinner was retained in the center of the new grille. Unlike GM cars, which had masses of chrome, all Fords were conspicuous by the absence of chrome. Although only one convertible was offered in the entire Ford range, it was a new one. Called the Sunliner, it sold for $2,027. There was just one convertible in Mercury's Monterey series, none in the Custom line. It was totally different from the 1949–51 Mercury, which pretended it was a baby Lincoln: now it decided to be a big Ford, with which it shared body panels. Dressed up in a light color and wide whites, the convertible was very stylish. More than five thousand soft-tops were built, small change compared to Ford's more than twenty-

two thousand units in the same period. Incidentally, Ford was the leading producer of convertibles in America, if not the world.

Like its lesser brethren, Lincoln had a total redesign in 1952. It was also the first Ford product to receive a brand-new, valve-in-head V8. The three Ford makes shared many design similarities, and they were all handsome automobiles, particularly the convertibles. As for Lincoln, a new model, the Capri, became the marque's top car, and offered Lincoln's single convertible. With the new ball-joint front suspension, the first to be offered by any make, the Lincoln was a very roadable, comfortable car in any guise. Liberal sound-deadening made the convertible whisper-quiet compared to other makes, and the slanted, curved windshield helped the wind flow smoothly round the car. Only 1,191 convertibles were built, a fraction of arch-rival Cadillac's 6,400.

In 1953, the Korean War finally ended. At home, wraparound windshields had come into vogue, thanks to the special Cadillac Eldorado convertible and Oldsmobile Fiesta convertible. Flashily beautiful is the only way to describe the three limited-edition convertibles. They were Harley Earl styles, from their rounded hoods to their fleshy rear fenders and, in the case of two of them, their "chopped" wraparound windshields. Only the Buick Skylark stuck with a normal frontal glass area, which was also cut down. Every option was included in these swanky convertibles, which cost from $5,000 (for the Skylark) to $7,750 (for the super Caddy). Consequently, the Buick sold 1,690, the Eldorado 532, and the $5,717 Fiesta only 458. At these prices, it was obvious these delightful convertibles would sell only to America's nouveaux riche and Hollywood celebrities, not to the old-money classes who remained tastefully reserved. Apart from the Robert Bourke–designed '53 Studebaker, which was a styling tour de force, the three GM cars were the best-looking of the year.

Something new was offered to Americans in 1953. It was white, with a red interior and two seats. It was the first Chevrolet Corvette. Harley Earl admired European and British sports cars and noted that other Americans did, too. MGs and Jaguars had carved a niche that Earl thought should have an American presence. He and chief engineer Ed Cole began to design a sports car that would wave the Stars and Stripes. Once the ball was rolling, Cole's Chevrolet engineering staff and Earl's Art & Color

Studio were told to produce a viable fiberglass sports car. A blend of American and European influences went into the first Corvette, which premiered as a show car at New York's glitzy Motorama in 1953. It went into production shortly after and, although only 315 were produced, and it was almost axed, Corvette survived to become Chevrolet's flagship, a world-class sports car, largely through the inspiration and untiring effort of chief engineer Zora Arkus-Duntov. The Corvette did not become a true convertible until 1956, when it replaced its plastic side curtains with glass windows.

For the first time in a number of years, Studebaker didn't have a convertible in 1953. It's interesting to speculate how the stunning car would have looked without a top—likely very European and very elegant. At this time, Studebaker was facing major financial problems. Sales, even with the beautiful styling, were declining way below the break-even point.

Packard, on the other hand, was healthy and had money: not much, but enough to keep its head above water. As if to prove a point, Packard introduced a new model, the decidedly sharp Caribbean convertible. It looked very like the 250 Mayfair convertible introduced a year earlier and was, in fact, part of the Mayfair group. Two convertibles on the same 122-inch (309.8cm) wheelbase might sound confusing. Both had the same body bumpers and grille, but there the similarities ended. One look at the

ABOVE LEFT: *The 1954 Corvette was still a roadster and not yet a convertible: wind-up windows came in 1956. Poor performance and equally poor sales had Chevrolet and GM wondering whether to shelve the sports car project. Fortunately, they didn't, and the Corvette became the world-class sports car it is today.*

ABOVE: *In 1953, Buick, Cadillac, and Oldsmobile each produced a special, limited edition model. They were, of course, based on the same platform, yet managed to look quite different from each other. Here is the Oldsmobile Fiesta, of which only 458 were produced.*

Caribbean was enough to set it apart from the herd; this convertible was all glamour. There was a difference in price, too: the Caribbean sold for $5,210, the standard convertible for $3,486. Full chrome-edged wheel arches complemented the otherwise trim-free Caribbean sides, in contrast to the jagged brightwork adorning the standard model, whose rear wheels were almost completely closed. The hoods were different, too. Unlike the standard model, the Caribbean's hood was devoid of cormorants and chrome; it had a full-width, non-functioning air scoop instead. A 327 L-8 power plant developing 180 horsepower gave the Caribbean a comfortable cruising speed, but it was unable to touch Cadillac, Lincoln, or Chrysler for get-up-and-go. The days of the old side valve motors were numbered. By 1955, they disappeared into the wide blue yonder.

Buick, Cadillac, and Oldsmobile rebodied their cars in 1954, and the Cadillac series 62 convertible was longer, lower, and wider. Horsepower was raised to 230 as the horsepower race got underway. Wheelbases of all Cadillacs were lengthened to accommodate the extra inches. There were only two convertibles: the Series 62 and the Eldorado. The Eldorado did

better in 1954, selling 2,150 units, a considerable increase from the year before. But the standard Series 62 convertible was a smart-looking automobile, selling more than 6,300 copies. All Cadillacs sported panoramic windshields. (A little-known singer-cum-truck-driver who liked comic-book hero Captain Marvel, Jr., had an ambition to own a Cadillac convertible one day. His name was Elvis Presley.)

Also very handsome was the 1954 Oldsmobile 98 Starfire convertible. Like Cadillac, it featured a wraparound windshield. Flashy two-color combinations were becoming the latest fad, and were nicely done on the Starfire. Buick, as always, had the most convertibles, one for each series. The Super was very attractive; the quiet, conservative design was handsome without being gaudy. For most of its existence, Buick has built convertibles that feel solid and secure. As its slogan used to say, "When better cars are built, Buick will build them."

Face-lifts made up most of the rest of the 1954 offerings, but, once again, there were curious exceptions. One was the Nash (or Hudson, since the two companies merged in 1954) Metropolitan. The brainchild of free-lance stylist Bill Flajole, who designed a car based on the Fiat 500 chassis, it interested Nash chief George W. Mason and Nash engineer Meade F. Moore enough to take the design onboard. Development of the tiny car continued, with the idea that Fiat should produce it. That idea didn't work out; it was thought Fiat wasn't reliable enough, so the job of building the little car went to England's Austin. Although a completely American design (to save costs), Austin's perky four-cylinder, 73.8-cubic-inch (1,209.3 cubic cm) engine was utilized. At a time when Americans were taught that bigger was better, the Metropolitan did extremely well. There were two models: a three-passenger coupé and three-passenger convertible. It was a cute little car, and the convertible was especially nice. As a first car for a struggling young married couple, it was an ideal way to enjoy the pleasures of open-air motoring without worrying too much about the monthly payments.

Besides the mergers (Studebaker with Packard, Nash with Hudson), independent automaker Kaiser-Frazer bit the dust in 1955. While they continued selling leftover cars in 1955, that was the end; Frazer's last car had been made in 1949. Neither produced a convertible, which was a pity

ABOVE: *Cadillac grilles evolved rather than making a complete change. A simple eggcrate pattern replaced the heavy but elegant chrome bars. This is a 1954 Cadillac Eldorado convertible coupé, which was more like a production line Cadillac than in 1953.*

ABOVE RIGHT: *The interior of the 1954 Cadilac Eldorado sported a two-tone wheel and seats and a dash loaded with chrome. These flashy elements appealed to more than two thousand buyers and attracted the attention and affection of future rock star Elvis Presley.*

LEFT: *Harley Earl loved European sports cars, and after a 30-month development program between Harley's Art & Color Studio and Chevrolet, the Corvette became a reality. The body was fiberglass (and remains so to this day) and the engine an anemic six-cylinder Blue Flame Six that didn't excite anybody, least of all the Corvette.*

RIGHT: *After years of staid, old-fashioned looking cars, stylist Virgil Exner lifted Chrysler Corporation back into the present with a series of beautiful cars gleefully advertised as the "Forward Look." The 1955 Dodge was mainly the work of Exner employee Murray Baldwin, as was the little-changed 1956 model shown here. Paint and chrome adorned the hood in an interesting trim pattern that extended along the sides of the car.*

BELOW: *Twin pods inserted into the rear fender and surrounded by chrome trim on the 1955 Dodge Lancer served as eye-catching decorative function at its best.*

considering the Kaiser's attractive styling. The only open car was the two-passenger Kaiser Darrin. Designed by Dutch Darrin and built in the company's final year, the fiberglass Darrin had unique sliding doors and a landau top with a halfway-up position. Of course, the Darrin was not a convertible, but a roadster, for it had no side windows, only plastic curtains. Unfortunately, with Kaiser going under, the Darrin lasted only one season.

Chrysler's market share had plummeted to 13 percent of the total, and Virgil Exner had been taken on to try to save Chrysler with completely new and modern styling. Exner was too late to do much with the 1954

crop, but what he did do made the cars look better than they had for some time. There was a smart midyear Dodge convertible called the Royal 500, the numbers signifying Dodge had been the Indianapolis 500 Pace Car for 1954. As a racing competitor, Dodge was doing extremely well. Twin sedans and convertibles powered by Red Ram OHV V8s, which were smaller hemis than Chrysler's, set 196 AAA certified speed records during the month of September 1953, at Bonneville. Chrysler V8s also took five of the first six places in the Pan American Road Race. In 1954, 701 factory-built Pace Car replicas were sold, all of them convertibles.

The boom year of 1955 was the gateway to the future: everything was coming up roses in the economy, new homes were selling in record numbers, unemployment was low. As for the car industry, it never had such a good year. Reflecting the public's mood, virtually every car was all-new in

1955 and, while there was no change in the number of convertible models, new styling and colors made it seem that there were more. There were brand-new V8 engines, new suspensions, two- and three-tone colors—new everything.

There was something for everybody, including two new cars to rave about. One, the hot and haughty Chrysler C-300 letter series, was a thinly disguised NASCAR racer prepared for the street. The other was Ford's exciting two-seat Thunderbird. Both cars were beautiful, true works of automotive art. Unfortunately, the 300 didn't have a convertible version; that would follow later. But the Thunderbird was all convertible, with a choice of hardtop or soft. While many refer to the Thunderbird as Ford's answer to the Corvette, a two-seater had actually been floating around Ford design studios for a number of years, according to Frank Hershey. It was Hershey, and the Ford design team working under him, who were responsible for Thunderbird's classic shape. (Incidentally, the Red Indian totem pole emblem was influenced by a huge design seen on the walls of Phoenix Airport.) Under the forward-tilting hood lay a 292-cubic-inch (4,785 cubic cm) V8 rated at 193 bhp with a manual transmission, 198 if automatic.

Its simple crosshatch grille behind an equally simple bumper carrying bumper guards shaped like the Ford grille spinner, its heavily hooded headlights, sharply curved wraparound windshield, attractively designed hood scoop, and two-toned interior blended into a design regarded then and now as one of the best styling jobs ever done on an American car. Though a two-passenger automobile, Ford declined to call the T-Bird a sports car. Instead it was referred to as a "personal car," a coy interpretation thought up by some public relations employee. As everybody said the T-Bird was Ford's answer to Chevy's Corvette, and the Corvette was more of a sports car, Ford obviously wanted to differentiate the two. So a "per-

sonal car" the T-Bird became. Having the look of a scaled-down Ford Sunliner convertible—the family resemblance was no accident—at the time, the Thunderbird was a better image-builder than the Corvette was for Chevrolet, though that would change beginning with the V8 offered in 1955. That the T-Bird scored is immediately apparent by comparing its and the Corvette's 1955 sales figures: there were 16,155 Thunderbirds and 674 Corvettes produced.

Chevrolet and Plymouth joined Ford in offering new OHV V8 engines in 1955. Styling was fresh and new, and the Chevrolet was particularly distinguished. The stylists under Harley Earl had produced a classic but simple design, which still makes many who see it skip a heartbeat to

ABOVE: *Famed car designer Franklin Hershey designed the "Silver Streaks" adorning the hood of the 1950 Pontiac Chieftain; they first appeared in 1935 and remained through 1956. A 108 bhp straight-eight was the buyers' first choice, although the venerable straight-six was standard.*

LEFT: *The crescent-shaped mph counter surrounded by round dials was the 1950 Pontiac Chieftain's approach to instrumentation. Note the Indian chief on the steering wheel hub. The Indian had been with Pontiac since the beginning, but disappeared after 1956.*

this day. From the pure but elegant Ferrari-like, egg-crate grille, to the notched waistline, the beautiful two-tone combinations to the simple taillights, there were few cars so shapely, so desirable as the 1955 Chevrolet. A Bel-Air convertible sporting a 265 Ed Cole–designed V8 (one of the best ever to hit the market), power steering, power brakes, Powerglide transmission, and, naturally, an AM radio was an instant classic, a masterpiece of automotive design.

The Chevy faced some pretty tough competition in 1955; the new Plymouth with its bold Exner styling was a real standout. Besides styling, Plymouth was given V8 power for the first time. In convertible form (there was only the Belvedere), the car's unique side trim and slanted back wraparound windshield added luster to the already handsome body.

In answer to Chevrolet's Corvette, Ford introduced the two-seater Thunderbird in 1955. Termed a "personal car" by Ford, the Thunderbird won accolades for its beauty. The above is the little-changed 1956 version, which could be had with a lift-off hardtop roof, for which two people were needed to accomplish the removal, or a standard convertible top. The porthole first appeared in 1956.

Another real beauty was Chrysler's New Yorker convertible. This was Exner styling at its best, and its heady claim to the "Hundred-Million-Dollar Look" may have been brash even if beyond contention. Here is what Tom McCahill, America's finest and funniest automobile guru, said when he tested the New Yorker convertible for *Mechanix Illustrated*: "Power plant-wise these can be described as detuned Chrysler 300s, the hairy-chested, two-fisted rip-snorter that was designed for the male of the family who desired a competition bucket in houseboat size." A couple of paragraphs later, McCahill said the car was "one of the finest handling big American cars I have ever driven." He qualified this by saying its ride was too soft and needed the heavier suspension under the sporty 300. "What this car needs, in my opinion, is guttier shocks and springs," he said.

Finally, McCahill said of the $3,924 convertible: "Of all the high priced cars on the American market today, almost every part of a Chrysler looks as though it cost more than any corresponding part on the competition's offerings." Despite McCahill's endorsement of the New Yorker convertible, only 946 were produced, even in a banner year like 1955. Costing $834 less was the Windsor convertible, which sold a little better, with 1,395 units built.

Now erroneously merged with Studebaker, cash-strapped Packard couldn't do better than a major face-lift. But what a face-lift; it was a small miracle, considering every possible obstacle was facing the once-great company. Briggs built Packard bodies, but sold out to Chrysler in 1954. Chrysler coldly informed Packard that Briggs would no longer be supplying bodies to the struggling company, which then needed all the help it could get. Therefore, Packard was reduced to building cars in a tiny body plant on Corner Avenue, Detroit. Consequently, there were many production delays leading to severe quality control problems on the superb-looking 1955 cars. Despite everything piling up against it, Packard produced what were undoubtedly the most advanced cars of the decade.

Dick Teague, one of the great car designers, worked in Packard styling from 1951 until the end, and he was responsible for the last great Packards of 1955–56. His jewel was the Caribbean convertible, a car at one with the mid-fifties' mode. It sported a wraparound windshield, peaked front fenders, a massive grille, Cadillac-style bumpers, three-tone colors, and wire wheels. It was as elegant as the taste of the fifties demanded, truly the rebirth of a great and honorable name. Very fast, with safe handling, the Caribbean was one of the great sunshine cars of the decade.

It had panache and always attracted stares, whether traveling at high speed or rolling up to the country club. It cost $5,932, yet only five hundred were built. Reversible seat-cushion covers (leather one side, cloth the other) were a special plus for Packard's beautiful Caribbean, not that they did much good; in 1956, a paltry 276 units were built. Packards took a real nosedive in 1956 due to the problems encountered with 1955 models. As noted earlier, these problems were soon ironed out, though buyer resistance remained.

This new Packard had Torsion-Level suspension consisting of interlinked torsion bars operating on all four wheels. The torsion bars would automatically adjust electronically for load weight, resulting in one of the best rides in the automobile field. It didn't end there: Packard joined the OHV V8 club by introducing an oversquare unit displacing 320 cubic inches (5,243.8 cubic cm) on Clipper DeLuxe and Super models, and

DeSoto fitted in the Chrysler scheme of things between Dodge and Chrysler, possibly closer to the latter than it should have. DeSoto and Chrysler competed against each other, their medium price structure overlapping, much to the detriment of DeSoto. Introduced in 1930, DeSoto went to the wall in 1961. The car shown is a decorative 1956 DeSoto Fireflite convertible coupé.

352 inches (5,768.2 cubic cm) on Clipper Customs, Packards, and the Caribbean.

Cadillac, whose styling was loved by Elvis and hated by motoring doyen Tom McCahill (he said it was the car to haul the groceries in), had two convertibles, both in the 62 Series. There were 12,100 convertibles produced in 1955; 3,950 Eldorados. Small fins continued on all Cadillacs

except the Eldorado; those were longer, razor-edged, and sat above two round taillights merged into a tubular protuberance that extended above the rear wheel arch. Huge pointed dagmars (so called after the features of a well-endowed actress named Dagmar) jutted out from the V-shaped, egg-crate grille, and color-harmonized leathers decorated the jazzy interior. The Eldorado was Cadillac's top convertible, and was priced at $6,286, more than $300 above the more elegant Packard.

In record-breaking 1955, 10,668 Mercury Montclair convertibles were made. Like Ford, the Mercury had an all-new body, wraparound windshield, hooded headlights similar to Packard's, and a massive bumper/grille assembly comprising two thick horizontal bars joined together by three heavy-looking vertical ones. Dagmars completed the brutish look. Chrome was the big thing in 1955, and Mercury had more than its fair share. Nevertheless, the convertible had a certain appeal that shouted, "Let's rock 'n' roll."

ABOVE TOP: *The 1957 Chrysler Corporation cars were designer Virgil Exner's crowning achievement. Long, lithe, and truly beautiful, Chrysler products took the styling lead away from GM. As sunshine cars go, the 1957 Chrysler New Yorker was a dream come true.*

ABOVE BOTTOM: *Fins tall as skyscrapers touched the heavens. Look at the beautiful taillight design that is so simple yet very stylish. Pushbutton TorqueFlite automatic transmission, front torsion bar suspension, and a hemi V-8 made all Chrysler cars the safest, best handling vehicles in America.*

RIGHT: *Plymouth was Chrysler's answer to Ford and Chevrolet, and had been since 1928. In convertible form, the 1957 Plymouth Belvedere was affordable enough to allow anybody to let the sunshine in on the escape road to romance.*

More than anything, rock 'n' roll was convertible music, Mercury music, Ford Sunliner music, Elvis Presley music. Besides music, one of Presley's interests was the automobile. Big, flashy, chrome-laden automobiles, Cadillacs especially. He loved the big convertible Caddies of the mid-fifties—in fact, any Cadillac. Once he hit the big time, Elvis bought a 1955 pink Cadillac sedan he promptly gave to his mother. Over the years, Elvis bought one hundred Cadillacs, but most of his convertibles were foreign jobs, though he kept a 1955 or 1956 Cadillac convertible in his spacious garage.

Even if Elvis and his swiveling hips hadn't been around, 1955 was still an outrageous year. In automotive terms, it was a year to remember: 9,188,574 vehicles were built, of which well over 7 million were cars, a world record. Nineteen fifty-six calmed down a bit; after all, those 7 million cars still had quite a bit of life left in them, and the new cars were mostly face-lifts. Still, production was 5.8 million, the fourth highest in the history of the American automobile.

Chrysler had chrome caps on the rear fenders in 1955 that could be described as embryonic fins; in 1956, all Chrysler products had fins. They were small compared with what was to come, but fins nonetheless. A 1956 Chrysler convertible was extremely attractive, its fins giving it a look of dartlike motion. But the best-looking convertible that year had to be the brand-new Lincoln Premiere. Running a very poor second behind Cadillac, Ford decided Lincoln would require a major upgrade to attract customers. This

was in 1952, when Bill Schmidt, Lincoln-Mercury's chief stylist since the mid-forties, presented to upper management a full-sized clay model of a car more competitive than the then-current Mexican Road Race–winning Lincoln. At the same time, the company decided to revive the Lincoln Continental as a car considerably above the Cadillac in stature. Viewing the clay, it was agreed by all present that this was to be the basis for the 1956 Lincoln.

The new Continental Mark II was a beautiful car, defying America's baroque taste with quiet, classic styling in the Rolls-Royce or Mercedes mode. There was only one model, a two-door hardtop coupé. Virtually hand-built, the Continental upstaged Cadillac, but only for a year, as Cadillac had its Brougham in the wings. The company spent $100 million on developing the new Lincoln, and the result showed the money was well

GM went on a chromium plate binge culminating in cars like the striking 1957 Pontiac Star Chief convertible coupé. Chrome was everywhere, though it was not quite as bad as the 1958 models that practically emptied Rhodesia's (Zimbabwe's) chrome mines. Massive grille, pods, and bumpers were jukebox technology that worked.

spent. When the 1956 Lincoln appeared, it became the first car ever to win the Industrial Designers Institute award for automotive design. This was a well-deserved feather in Bill Schmidt's cap. The 1956 Lincoln was arguably one of the finest-looking cars of the decade, yet collectors today ignore it for the most part.

Lincoln had only one convertible, the Premiere. All new in 1956, the Lincoln relied on a face-lift that included stacked dual headlights (the lower ones served as auxiliary lights, since not all states had written proper duals into law), and the suggestion of razor-edged fins. From the waterfall sculpturing along the sides, the hooded headlights, the massive horizontal grille bisected by the bumper, to the low rear fenders, the Premiere looked and felt like a quality automobile. Its lazy 368-cubic-inch (6,030.4 cubic cm) V8 pulled along effortlessly, turning in 0-to-60 times of eleven seconds. According to "Uncle" Tom McCahill, the Lincoln had enough power and torque to "yank the Empire State Building up by its roots."

For most, the good life continued to be good. Detroit's war of attrition among the auto companies went from strength to strength. Studebaker-Packard's merger was ultimately fatal, while Nash-Hudson's marriage to become American Motors would eventually prove quite successful. Chrysler, after a tremendous 1955, fell back in 1956, but rumors around Motown spoke of radical new cars for 1957. Ford, too, became an object of intense interest for spy cameras near the proving ground. Car companies traditionally brought out all-new models every three or four years, although the bodies might be face-lifted during the model run.

In the quest to be ahead of everyone else, all this changed in the mid-fifties. Planned obsolescence with a vengeance became the order of the day, and Ford and Chrysler started the ball rolling. If 1955 had been an exciting year for car buyers, 1957 would prove to be a heart-stopper. Those were the days when there was a human edge to Detroit's relationship with customers. The motor companies pandered to the millions itching for the annual circus by announcing shiny bright new cars "now at your dealer." Small boys got caught up in the excitement, sometimes

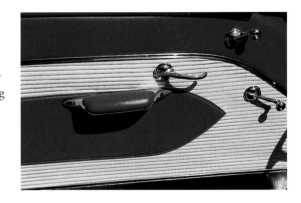

sneaking out at night to watch for the big car haulers delivering the latest, greatest, completely unbelievable, stunningly new cars.

After 1955, how different could the cars get? Very different, especially Chryslers and Fords. When the wraps were taken off the 1957 Fords, there was a sharp intake of breath. Nobody quite expected what they saw; as we have already seen, cars had a three-year life cycle and here was Ford with all-new models after only two. There was no single designer responsible for the '57 cars. Bill Boyer of Ford's advanced styling studio, Frank Hershey, L. David Ash, Bob McGuire, and others all contributed to the new models. At the end of the day, design VP George Walker would give the designs a once-over, perhaps changing here, altering there. Although the new cars were truly handsome, their styling heralded the coming "design by committee" age.

Whether one or many designers worked on the 1957 Fords is a moot point. What came out of the studios shocked GM to the quick. The world's number one automaker had traditionally relied on a third-year face-lift, albeit a heavy one to make their cars look as new as possible. No such problem with Ford; the cars were new. Ford had two wheelbases of 116 and 118 inches (294.6 and 299.7cm), and the fleet Sunliner convertible sat on the larger one. Although the larger Fairlanes and Sunliners featured two-tone paint, their design was clean-cut and square-edged. Front fenders were flattened on top, the hood was narrower and opened forward, thus allowing more room in the engine bay, and the rectangular grille had a clean, purposeful look. Under the flat-top, hooded fenders, sat single headlights in protruding pods; the flattened fenders were prepared to take the soon-to-come dual headlights once they were ratified by all the states. The Sunliner, equipped with the 312-cubic-inch (5112.7 cubic cm), four-barrel V8 rated at 245 hp, was no slouch, hitting sixty mph (96kph) in 9.5 seconds from rest.

Improvements to the suspension helped handling, but it was the car's profile that made people sit up and take notice. There were fins. Small, perhaps, but fins nevertheless. They were accented by a sweeping side spear

ABOVE: *Compared to the delicate taillight assembly featured on Chryslers, Pontiac chose ornate designs chromed to excess. Exhausts exit through bumper tips.*

ABOVE RIGHT: *Even Pontiac's interior design was flashy in a Wurlitzer kind of way. The door was a mass of chrome that reflected everything that came by.*

of chrome with a gold anodized insert sandwiched between the first three-quarters of the car. The final quarter accentuated the slightly canted fins that ended in large, rounded taillights. There were two Ford convertibles in 1957, and the second one was very special indeed. That was the retractable Fairlane Skyliner, an incredibly long car—it was three inches (7.6cm) longer than other Fairlanes—in which the all-steel roof slid into the gargantuan trunk at a touch of a button. And that trunk was enormous—when the roof was up, that is. But when the roof was down, of course, it practically filled the trunk, leaving just enough room for an overnight toothbrush and possibly a toothpick. If the family was going on holiday, the top stayed up.

Somehow the Skyliner fitted in with America's tireless energy, its need to progress, to invent new mechanical marvels one year and make them obsolete the next with something newer and better. Considering what went into making the Skyliner practical, the car was a marvel. Under the sleek, somewhat rear end-heavy body were six hundred feet (182.8m) of wiring, eight circuit breakers, ten power relays, three motor drives, and ten limit switches that combined to make the roof perform its eye-catching maneuver. (Nowadays the whole operation could be done with a computer chip.) America's vast motoring public stayed away from the Skyliner, no doubt worried lest one of the many relays or circuits have an off day, which is understandable.

Still, there were 20,766 Skyliners built in 1957, and the brave souls who owned them found they had an excellent car that gave little trouble. At $2,942, buyers had a bargain in the form of a unique convertible and a car to upstage the swish Cadillac convertible down the street. Ford still had some nice convertibles too: its Sunliner was a better-proportioned beauty, with the cloth top stowed away behind the rear seat, leaving enough trunk space to take a family of five on a two-week vacation. Same with the Lincoln Premiere.

A real eye-catcher, and a somewhat vulgar one at that, was the totally restyled Mercury. Tons of sculpturing and bags of chrome distinguished Ford's mid-priced offering, which ranged from $2,763 to $4,103. The latter figure was for the Turnpike Cruiser convertible. The Turnpike Cruiser was a completely new Mercury series in 1957, and was far more flamboyant than either the Monterey or Montclair models. All three series had convertibles, but the Turnpike Cruiser really stood out. It had a tucked-in rear roof and retractable rear window; a wrap-over, wraparound windshield that was flanked on either side by space-age air duct pods with fake aerials

sticking out of them. A gold anodized insert was applied to the sculptured, concave rear fender section. A larger, 345-cubic-inch (5,635.5 cubic cm) 290-bhp V8 equipped with a Holley four-barrel gave the Turnpike Cruiser

convertible peppy performance. A 255-bhp, 312-cubic-inch (5,112.7 cubic cm) V8 powered both the Monterey and Montclair, providing enough go to keep most owners happy. Still, even with three models, the Turnpike Cruiser only realized a 1957 production total of 16,761 units, and just 1,265 were convertibles. Obviously, many didn't care for the Mercury's outrageous styling and opted for an all-new, conservatively styled 1957 Oldsmobile or Buick instead. Longer, wider, and radically lowered, the new GM medium-priced cars sold almost three times as many cars as Mercury.

Nineteen fifty-seven was the last year for Ford's two-passenger "personal car," the Thunderbird. A major face-lift cost the T-Bird none of its

charisma, as Bill Boyer and his team exercised restraint in its final season. The exterior spare tire of 1955–56 was dropped into the trunk and, like its full-sized brethren, the T-Bird had mild fins. A total of 208 examples of the T-Bird were equipped with a $500 Paxton-McCulloch supercharger. The supercharger was offered because it was rumored Chevrolet's now very attractive Corvette would offer one (it didn't; instead the 'Vette had fuel injection). A T-Bird with the supercharger could run 0-to-60 times in under seven seconds, climaxing with a top speed of 125 mph (200kph) plus (a nice feature to have, if not oft used).

If Ford had tweaked GM's nose with its redesigned cars, then Chrysler must have delivered the knockout punch when it unveiled the most fantastic and beautiful sets of wheels to come out of anywhere. "Suddenly, it's 1960," crowed Chrysler's advertising copy, and people had to pinch themselves to see if they weren't dreaming. They weren't; in a year when Russia launched Sputnik, the world's first satellite, Chrysler showed off earthbound designs ripe for the new space age. The 1955 and 1956 Chrysler product designs by Virgil Exner had helped pull America's number three car company back into contention, but they were "teasers" compared with what was to come. Exner pulled out all the stops with deli-

ABOVE: *Up until 1955 the Imperial was Chrysler's top model. Then in 1955 it made a separate, distinct mark on its own. This 1957 Imperial Crown convertible boasts its own individual styling not shared with any other division. Movie buffs may remember Jayne Mansfield being driven around in one in the film* The Girl Can't Help It.

ABOVE LEFT: *"Gunsight" taillights became an Imperial trademark from 1955 through 1962. Shown here is the 1957 design.*

1957 was the final year for Ford's beautiful two-passenger Thunderbird. A modest restyling and the addition of small, canted fins gave the car a fresh look without detracting from its beauty. Again the detachable hardtop roof was offered.

ciously provocative, cleanly designed cars that made everything else look ten years behind. Of course, as everyone knows, the big news was the fins. Glorious fins, skyscraper fins soared almost as high as Sputnik's orbit. Gracefully swept-back windshields, fleet lines that gave them a look of perpetual motion, and road-holding comparable to many European sports cars gave Chrysler an edge that sent the opposition scrambling to the drawing boards. All Chrysler products were given torsion bar front suspension called "Torsion-Aire" in 1957. Coupled with stiffer, relocated rear leaf springs, a new Plymouth left Ford and Chevy chasing their own tails at a bend in the road. A Buick would wallow; a DeSoto rode flat. As for the exciting new Imperial convertible, it would leave Cadillac sniffling at the traffic lights. Imperial had been a top-of-the-line Chrysler model until 1955, when it became a separate marque competing directly with Cadillac

and Lincoln. Always a distant third to Cadillac, Imperial actually beat Lincoln into third place in calendar year production by the slimmest of margins (37,946 to 37,870). New car registrations showed Lincoln a little more than four thousand ahead. Compare both to Cadillac's 153,236 unit production! Still, the Imperial caused a few shocks here and there.

All Chrysler products, including the Imperial, had the superb new TorqueFlite 3-speed, push-button automatic transmission. There was no "Park" in the push-button mode; you yanked on the hand brake instead, a good practice now almost as extinct as the dinosaur. Then the Imperial had the hemi, as did Chrysler and DeSoto. The hemi was the hottest engine around in the correct state of tune. Tim Howley wrote a comparison report on Cadillac, Lincoln, and Imperial in issue 118 (August 1990) of the prestigious *Special Interest Autos* magazine. In the report, he remarks on the Imperial's handling superiority: "You can actually drive this brute at 50 mph into a 90 degree turn without either sliding or plowing or rear wheel breakaway," and "Cornering can almost be described as approaching that of a sports car of the era." *Motor Trend* magazine said much the same in its 1957 test, and Tom McCahill said it was, "The greatest car built in America ... the greatest big automobile I have ever driven in my life." High praise for a car 224 inches (568.9cm) long and eighty-one inches (205.7cm) wide.

The beautifully styled 1957 Chrysler New Yorker pleased *Motor Trend* testers with its superior handling and ride. But the convertible that drew the most looks after Ford's Skyliner had to be Chrysler's 300-C Letter Series car. A trapezoidal honeycomb grille not unlike a Type 166, 122, 340 Ferrari, distinguishes the 300-C from the New Yorker, as does the lack of chrome trim. Nineteen fifty-seven marked the first year the 300 got itself a convertible. An American thoroughbred if ever there was one, the 300-C convertible was the Grand Tourer to end all Grand Tourers. A 392-cubic-inch (6,423.7cubic cm) hemi developing either 375 or 390 bhp pushed the 300-C along to 140 mph (224kph) plus, easily posting 0-to-60 times in 7.9 to 8.5 seconds. Nestling behind the elegant steering wheel, behind the huge compound curved windshield, sitting on seats upholstered in top-quality leather, an array of functional instruments (sans idiot lights) arrayed in front of you, you know the 300-C convertible has true class. It also had the best riding and handling of any car made in America, even better than its lesser brethren. It was a truly magnificent automobile, the kind that comes along only once in a blue moon. Since it was never really meant to be much more than an image-builder, 300 Letter Series production was kept very low; only 2,402 were made in 1957 and just 484 of them were convertibles.

Naturally, Chrysler's other divisions jumped on the bandwagon, too. Plymouth had its Fury, all white with gold anodized trim, wheel covers, and grille. Called the Adventurer, DeSoto's special had a choice of two or three different hues and a convertible model as well. Dodge didn't really have a limited model; one could order a Coronet with a 354-cubic-inch

BELOW LEFT & RIGHT: *The glamorous 1958 Chevrolet convertible coupé was first offered in 1958. It replaced the Bel-Air as Chevy's top model.*

RIGHT: *It came, it saw, but it never conquered. In fact, the Edsel story reads like one of Shakespeare's tragedies. Market surveys conducted three years earlier suggested the public would buy a new medium-priced car. But the new marque was introduced during a recession year, at a time when the public wanted smaller cars, and its looks didn't go down too well. The odd, horseshoe collar grille became the butt of stand-up comedians' jokes. Edsel struggled for three years before Ford pulled the plug.*

(5,803.9 cubic cm) hemi, and it was called a D-500. (To confuse the issue, the hemi could be dropped into any Dodge model, provided you asked for a D-500, which had stiffer springs and shocks.) There were D-500 convertibles as well.

Motor Trend handed Chrysler its coveted Annual Achievement Award for superior handling and roadability in 1957, and rightly so. Chrysler products were the safest of any cars made in America at that time. But greatness came with a price that was to haunt Chrysler for many years to come: appalling construction quality and premature rusting. In the haste to get the cars out, nobody bothered with rust prevention or quality. Steering wheels came off the columns in the hands of owners; ball bearings turned to dust because somebody forgot to grease them; torsion bars snapped; Imperials even had rust on them when they left the factory. And so on, and so on.

Ford wasn't much better, but GM cars were very well put together. There are more 1957 Chevrolet Bel-Air convertibles in existence today than all Ford and Plymouth models put together. Chrysler's market share dropped dramatically in 1958, for which the company could only blame itself. To be fair, there was an economic downturn in 1958 that affected all motor companies. The mini-recession was particularly bad timing for Ford, whose eagerly awaited, all-new medium-priced car was announced. It was offered in four series on two wheelbases, but nobody could think of

1957 was the last year for the two-seater Thunderbird, and in 1958 Ford rolled out a new four-passenger version. There were cries of "foul" from the purists, but sales almost doubled, which made everyone at Ford very happy.

Pacer line, one in the Citation. Standard engine was a big 361-cubic-inch (5,915.7 cubic cm) V8, and tops was an enormous 410-cubic-inch (6,718.6 cubic cm) job pumping out 345 horses. The 0-to-60 time, incidentally, was around eight seconds, up there in Chrysler 300 range. Unlike almost everything else, the Edsel eschewed fins for a flat rear. Taillights were shaped like boomerangs, according to Tom McCahill, and there was sculpturing along the rear fenders. Twin bumpers flanked the controversial grille. With the exception of steering wheel and hub-mounted automatic transmission push buttons, the Edsel was a very conventional car. Its normality disappointed many who had expected something different, and the horseshoe collar grille didn't turn anybody on. The recession wore on, turning people away from the showrooms.

Ford had hoped to sell more than 100,000 Edsels in 1958, but managed only fifty thousand. Pacer convertibles racked up a mere 1,876 units. Only 930 Citation convertibles were produced. According to Tom McCahill, the handling was so-so. "In the big Citation I tested, at high speeds through rough corners, I found the suspension a little too horsebacky. In other words, it galloped when I didn't want it to gallop and was far too soft a ride for so much performance potential." Considering the car's potential, McCahill was right; Edsel engineers said there was an "export kit" that buyers could order, consisting of heavy-duty suspension components, for the car. "For my dough," McCahill wrote, "I wouldn't own one [Edsel] except with the export kit; without stiffer suspension, a car with so much performance could prove similar to opening a Christmas basket of King Cobras in a small room with the lights out." McCahill had a way with words that made him the nightmare of the motor companies.

Besides the Edsel, Ford had the new four-seater Thunderbird. Though the purists hated it, Ford Motor Company president and Ford Division chief Robert McNamara (later President Kennedy's Secretary of Defense) felt otherwise. The little T-Bird had done its job, but McNamara thought a four-seater luxury personal car would sell better, and he was right. Production almost doubled, from 21,380 in 1957 to 37,892 in 1958. Almost all were hardtops, but the convertible managed 2,134 units.

At 227 inches (576.5cm), the all-new, unit-bodied Lincoln beat everyone on the block for overall length. In a decade of longer, lower, wider, even this huge Lincoln was considered over the top. It was the largest unitized car ever made, a fact that initially met with a lot of opposition. When Ford decided to build a new plant in Wixom, Michigan, Lincoln was to share the same production lines with the new T-Bird, which was also unitized. Unit construction had long proved itself on small European cars as very strong and possessing a degree of rigidity that body-frame cars never had. The same applied to the big Lincoln and T-Bird; this form of construction helped enormously with convertible strength. Body flex is much reduced, thanks to outboard torque boxes and floorpan, which added stiffness that previously was only dreamed of. Canted dual headlights flowing into the grille, sculpted sides, and a massive, luxurious interior gave the quality-built convertible the look of an aircraft carrier. Yet the big Lincoln and its Continental Mark III clone handled extremely well, considering the elephantine girth. Those with fantasies of sailing the seven seas but no

a name. Poet Marianne Moore was hired to come up with a poetic-sounding name. Her Mongoose, Civique, and other none-too-poetic names displeased board chairman Ernie Breech, who apparently said, "Enough of all this. Let's call it the Edsel."

The Edsel was not as different as people supposed. In fact, the only thing distinctive about the car was the vertical grille, which became the butt of stand-up comedians' jokes. Some said the car looked as though it were sucking a lemon; others described the grille as a horseshoe collar; and other descriptions are too obscene to print here. On the smaller wheelbase (shared with Ford) were the Ranger and Pacer; on the larger one (Mercury), the Corsair and Citation. There was one convertible in the

Besides an all new, cleaner design, Buick also adopted new names. It was as if the designers wanted to erase all vestiges of the previous year, so the Roadmaster became the Buick Electra 225 in 1959. Canted front fenders were complemented by the rear fins. A more attractive grille had less chrome cubes than before. The right-hand fender-mounted rear view mirror is a rather amateurish add-on done later in the car's life.

PRECEDING PAGES: *The 1958 Buick Roadmaster wallowed in a sea of chrome: wherever there was space, chrome plate filled it. The grille consisted of 160 small chrome cubes within the monstrous chrome space. Many considered the car too ugly to own, and Buick's sales plummeted. Today however, these Buicks are collected as examples of the Rock 'n' Roll fifties in its purest form.*

ability to swim, need not have looked further than a 1958 Lincoln or Continental convertible.

Every car at GM was different in 1958, but all looked terrible. Only Chevrolet styling shone through the ranks of the worst-looking cars GM ever allowed out of the styling studios. After thirty years in the design hot

seat, Harley Earl's reign was approaching its end, and it was a shame it had to end with cars as bad as the 1958 crop. Earl's advice to his stylists—"go all the way and then back off"— obviously wasn't heeded, or maybe his age was telling. While the 1958 designs possessed all of Earl's favorite design ideals—rounded fenders, long profiles, feminine curves—the overall effect was as confused as the Mad Hatter's Tea Party. Chrome looked as though it had been laid on with a trowel. Once you got past the chrome rockets and spears slapped on indiscriminately all over the body, the new Pontiac was a handsome car. It had a nice, simple grille, quad headlights and, of course, Franklin Hershey's famous silver streaks were gone. Pontiac chief Bunkie Knudsen had ordered them removed from the 1957 models. If one liked the rocket emblem blazing along the sides, then the Bonneville convertible was the choice. Standard power was a 370-cubic-inch (6,063.1cubic cm), 255-horse V8, but for serious drivers of the open road, the fuel-injected 310-horsepower unit was the one to have.

Buick and Oldsmobile looked like the remains of a Republican convention: ultraconservative, but laden with baubles, bangles, and beads, or, in Buick's case, chrome. And baubles, too, if one counts the 160 chrome squares that made up Buick's grille. There were more rocket flutes along the side—GM's designers must have had a course in reading space-age literature—and the taillights were great, ungainly slabs of chrome. Although it would be impossible not to notice a 1958 Buick Century convertible, it did not appear to be the car of choice for politicians or movie folk to be noticed in. The problem was, the car was so noticeable in itself, who would look at the occupants?

If the Flint masterpiece was bad, look at what Lansing achieved with the Oldsmobile. This topped the Buick for vulgar excess by several degrees. Or would "yards" be a better word? The top-of-the-line 98 Series had acres of chrome plastered along the sides, front and rear. As for the rear bumpers and taillights, the design was a massive chromium artifact that defies any constructive criticism. In the Consumer Guide book, *The Complete History of General Motors*, authors Richard Langworth and Jan Norbye describe the 1958 Oldsmobile as "positively atrocious." Without a roof to help dilute some of the excess, the '58 convertible looks like something one might see being hawked on QVC today. It is so bad in fact, that its awfulness becomes quite desirable in a perverted sort of way. Both the 1958 Buick and Oldsmobile have become highly collectible, and there is little doubt that wherever one drives a 1958 Buick or Olds convertible, one is bound to be noticed.

Cadillac styling was as bad as the rest; in fact, it cheapened the car. However, the opposite was true of Chevrolet which, with the Pontiac, were the only redeeming features of GM's fall from styling grace. The new Impala model in convertible form was very attractive, the chrome gewgaws more tastefully applied. Here was a car that actually looked several notches above its lower-priced rivals.

America was getting tired of big, big, and bigger cars; in 1958, the only American-made car to post a sales increase was American Motors'

ABOVE: *Huge Cadillac tailfins outstripped anything Chrysler had to offer. Note the front grille theme was repeated in the rear. On the plus side, there were handling, suspension, and steering improvements, but as convertibles go, the 1959 Cadillac Series 62 was too big to be fun anymore.*

ABOVE LEFT: *Cadillac, once noted for graceful design and class, seemed to have completely lost its way by 1959. The loud interior went with the turquoise jewelry favored by the nouveaux riche. Obviously, this was the market late-fifties Cadillacs were catering to.*

At a time when Americans were buying more Volkswagens than ever before, Detroit kept pitching longer, lower, and much wider cars at them. To be fair, the garish 1959 Cadillac was designed at a time when Americans thought bigger was better. The overblown grille was made up of lines and bullet shaped protuberances, and the windshield wrapped over as well as around.

Although GM cars were cleaner, fleeter machines in 1959, the styling looked as though somebody had been reading too many comic books. Tailfins became huge bat wings on the 1959 Chevrolet Impala convertible and eyebrows graced the front.

Rambler. (There were no Rambler convertibles, by the way.) As the Big Three presented their 1959 crop of even bigger cars, the whisper against larger autos became a roar. Never mind that the recession eased and people started buying again, sales increases were more modest, with most of the increases not attaining 1957 levels.

Studebaker, having humiliated and killed off Packard in 1958—the final Packards were Studebakers with different grilles—brought out a compact model called the Lark. Using many components from the previous full-sized car, designer Duncan McRae created an attractive model that pushed Studebaker production from 18,850 in 1958 to 48,459 for 1959. American Motors did well in 1959 with smaller, practical designs; in 1961, the Rambler knocked Plymouth out of third place with a production total of almost half a million. But there were no convertibles in AMC's twenty-four models split into four series. There were plenty of convertibles over at the General's offices where, for the third time in three years, the models were all new. It was said that GM had earnings several times larger than a

number of European countries combined, and considering how much it would have cost to retool every year, this was probably true.

In any event, GM's 1959 crop reached for the stars with a series of outlandish designs that should have been orbiting the moon. Even though the '59 designs were radical, they would have been much worse had it not been for Bill Mitchell's influence. The cars were clean, smooth, and very sharp; they were generally wider and considerably longer, especially in the case of Chevrolet, whose length went up a staggering eleven inches (27.9cm) over 1958. All five divisions had convertibles as usual, though the Buick was perhaps the best-looking. It had fewer grille cubes than 1958, much cleaner, more angular lines, and the huge wrap-over, wrap-around windshield added greatly to the convertible. Canted front fenders, with accentuated trim along the tops, coursed downward along the side, and at the midway point, met the rear fenders that followed a similar line. Compared to 1958, chrome was applied sparingly, and the whole effect was one of motion.

Cadillac looked as though Salvador Dalí had been at it. Determined to out-fin Chrysler, Cadillac succeeded with the highest fins yet to grace a car. Rocket projections housing twin bullet-shaped taillights grew out of the fins, which, taking the car's ultraclean shape into consideration, looked ridiculous. The fins on the convertible looked top-heavy.

Chevrolet's convertible Impala was a jet-age wonder. Its fins didn't soar; they flopped over, gull-wing style. Beneath the fins rested the largest teardrop taillights imaginable. Once one had gotten over the shock, the Chevrolet was quite a desirable-looking car and definitely a fun way to travel with the top down and the old AM radio blasting out Jerry Keller's "Here Comes Summer."

GM stylists did everything they could to give each car a different set of fins. Pontiac got split fins and was regarded by many to be the General's best-looking car. As far as sales went, Pontiac was the only GM car to actually outdo 1957 production. As for Oldsmobile, it was the most conservative of the lot, with fins that hardly looked like fins. Unlike the others, the Olds had no real character, even in convertible guise. The hemi was gone, killed off by the Auto Manufacturers' Association following its ban on the industry's racing programs. Conventional wedge head engines filled the hemi's shoes.

Chrysler had sunk to an alarmingly small market share (about 12 percent), and the 1959 face-lifts didn't really help. The shark's fins grew larger on the Plymouth, making one think a Great White was close behind, but the rest of Chrysler's crop made do with grille and trim differences. Heaven knows what they did to the languishing DeSoto: the bumper/grille arrangement was clumsy and top-heavy. Best-looking by far was the clean-limbed 300E convertible. Only 140 300E convertibles were built, making this the second-rarest letter-series convertible of all. Only the 1962 300H convertible beat it for scarcity by seventeen units.

Perhaps the most striking convertible from Chrysler was the 1959 Dodge. There were two models, both on a 122-inch (309.8cm) wheelbase, the Coronet and the more expensive Custom Royal. Some argue it was the best-looking Dodge from the fifties, and it's hard to argue that it wasn't. An oval bumper/grille arrangement plus rakish, somewhat exaggerated brows over the headlights made sure nobody would mistake the Dodge for anything else. The fins were the same height, but even more rakish in style. An interesting option was the front swivel seats. Offered in all Chrysler products, at the touch of a side-mounted lever the seats swung outward, thus allowing women wearing skirts to exit the car gracefully.

Power was the item manufacturers still thought sold cars in 1959, and they shoveled it under the hoods by the bucketful. Dodge boasted a 383 equipped with four-barrel carburetors that developed 345 bhp. There was a huge 413-cubic-inch (6,767.8 cubic cm) mill putting out 380 horses in the mighty 300E. Cadillac was offering 325 and 345 bhp from its 390 V8, and even Chevrolet had a 348, with horsepower ranging from 250 to 315. Some were beginning to question the necessity of all this power, especially in cars that hadn't, with the exception of Chrysler, the handling to match.

Once again, it was Ford that had the convertible to end all convertibles. Because he thought the car frivolous, McNamara axed the retractable Skyliner after only three seasons. The third-season one was the best looking: Ford's 1959 design won the Gold Medal for Exceptional Styling at the Brussels World Fair. Both the conventional Sunliner and the retractable Skyliner were very desirable convertibles; there were 45,868 Sunliners and 12,915 Skyliners built. In its three years there were 48,394 Skyliners produced, a figure almost equaled in one year by the 1959 Sunliner.

In the upper-crust market, Lincoln's convertible was hardly changed, save for a less-pronounced front fender concave. Over at Mercury, it was an all-new look. Longer, lower, a massive compound curved windshield, body sculpturing that extended into the front doors, and a honeycomb grille highlighted the car, which could be had with a colossal 430-cubic-inch (7,046.4 cubic cm) V8. As for Edsel, nobody wanted it. Drastic face-lifting didn't help. Only the Ranger, Corsair, and a couple of wagons were offered. There was a Corsair convertible, though not many bothered with it (1,343 were built) when they could have a very similar Ford for less money.

One of the greatest decades of the twentieth century was over. It was a decade of opposites, a time of positive advance on one hand, negative thought on the other. As for the cars, well, tremendous strides were made in engineering, but it was the decade of the stylist, who created art forms on wheels. There will never again be a car like the 1957 Chrysler, the 1953 Buick Skylark, or the 1959 Ford Skyliner. All were incredible, unbelievable machines that bucked convention in much the same way Salvador Dali, Jackson Pollock, and Andy Warhol turned their backs on the establishment. After the fifties, the sixties would shock and enlighten. Some would look back, shake their heads, and say: "What now, my love?"

Ford's 1959 models were extremely handsome, well-designed cars that won the Gold Medal for Exceptional Styling at the Brussels (Belgium) World Fair. For $2,839, one could have sunshine fun in the Galaxie Sunliner shown here.

"TUNE IN, TURN ON, DROP OUT"

—Timothy Leary (1921–1996)

The change between 1959 and 1960 was acute; Detroit had noticed long before others and was prepared. The auto industry was pretty adept at gauging the fickle tastes of the public, though it needed to be pushed on occasion.

Such an occasion was the increasing interest in smaller cars. People were tiring of the constant annual changes: more fins, more chrome, and more color. Studebaker and American Motors proved it with their steady-selling compact Lark and Rambler American models. Naturally, the independents couldn't keep this fast-growing market to themselves; the Big Three announced their compacts for 1960. None were convertibles to start with.

LEFT: *The Industrial Designers Institute rarely hands out awards to the auto industry, but in June 1961, they made an exception when they awarded Lincoln the prize for "an outstanding contribution of simplicity and design elegance." The IDI was referring to the beautiful 1961 Lincoln Continental.*

Chrysler fielded the European-looking Plymouth Valiant, Ford its very conventional Falcon, and Chevrolet its radical, very advanced, rear-engine Corvair. Each car was attractively styled, sensibly sized, and economical to run.

More changes appeared in 1961; the way things were going, it began to look like the fifties all over again. Admittedly, the new styling was quieter and more conservative, but there was change in abundance, though not at Chrysler. Giving a new body to a unitized car every year would have been a costly, unnecessary business and something Chrysler couldn't afford. Still, the company managed extensive face-lifts, and for some curious reason, Exner flipped Dodge's tail fins in the opposite direction. Sculptured curves, odd front fenders, a strange grille and roof were Plymouth's lot—it really was ugly. The convertible looked like several cars blended together, for there was no continuity of line, just a mess.

Chrysler's big news was unitized body construction across the board. Unibody construction consisted of a stamped steel body welded to a channel section steel frame. A front subframe was utilized for engine and suspension. Unit construction was nothing new; many European cars had used it for years. In America, Nash had used unit construction since 1941 and Hudson since 1948, hence American Motors' reliance on the system. There is little doubt about the advantages of unit construction: more rigidity, and better stress absorption, and, with added rust prevention, a unitized structure is a stronger and safer way to build convertibles.

Chrysler's 1960 styling continued to adhere to the finny school of thought, but Chrysler designers seemed to have lost their way. The cars looked confused and disjointed. Although convertibles are generally handsome, romantic cars, nobody could say this with any conviction about Chrysler cars. Although sales were up, there was a death in the family: after thirty-two years, DeSoto, following several years of poor sales, bit the dust after very few 1961 models were made.

Another family suffered a bereavement as well; after a short, unhealthy life, the unfortunate Edsel followed the DeSoto. Gone was its vertical grille, to be replaced by twin horizontal ones that looked as though a 1959 Pontiac had been around. Merely a clone of the 1960 Ford, the Edsel Ranger convertible was still quite a handsome car. Only seventy-six convertibles were made out of a total 2,846 units, and they are highly collectible nowadays—if you can find one. Watch out for fakes: unscrupulous vendors have been known to turn a 1960 Ford into a 1960 Edsel.

Studebaker offered a convertible Lark for the first time in 1960. The biggest engine was the 195-horsepower, 259.2-cubic-inch (4,2475.1 cubic cm) V8. The Lark convertible was ideal for young couples, but no good for families of five.

GM had new bodies and three extra compacts in 1961, one for each division except Cadillac. None were convertibles. Wraparound windshields were gone except on the big Cadillac Series 75, and all cars reflected Mitchell's styling influences. There was a lot of sculpturing, less chrome, and, with the exception of Cadillac, no fins. All the convertibles were attractive, clean-looking cars, but there was nothing memorable about them. One of the best-looking cars to come out of the fifties was the ill-fated 1956–57 Lincoln Continental Mark II. This beautiful car was the

barometer for good taste in American design, yet it didn't sell. It was, well, just too good. Nor did the Edsel sell, as we all know. Both cars died, the Edsel in 1961, the Mark II after two seasons. Then came George Walker's 1958–60 behemoths, a total contradiction to the Mark II.

Lincoln/Mercury had already decided on a new approach to the Continental more in keeping with the Mark II. Originally, the 1961 Continental was designated to be the new Thunderbird. Bob Thomas, a senior Ford stylist, worked on the 1961 Continental: "We were given the job of a T-Bird that was supposed to look like a Continental. I don't know why we were given that job, but we were." In an interview given to *Continental Comments*, the Lincoln Continental Owners Club magazine in 1983, Bob Thomas said Robert McNamara saw the T-Bird clay and suggested it should be the Continental. "'We were going berserk in design," remembered Bob. "So I talked to Elwood Engel, chief of advanced styling, and told him engineering was only interested in the width at the cowl." Engineering didn't want the revised T-Bird package to be wider at the front. "I said to Engel," continued Bob, "'Now if we take that car and pull out the back end, we can get a wide, low-looking back end on this thing. And we can set the top like the Mark II.' And Elwood went along and said, 'Let's do it.' So we had this beautiful back end that was terrific."

Not only the rear but the whole car was terrific, an instant classic in the correct sense of the word. Two models were announced for 1961: a four-door sedan and a four-door convertible. According to Thomas, Engel followed the Continental through to its completion, adding his trademark razor-edged fender peaks, to which he attached a stainless steel molding. Although pioneered by the 1957 Imperial, curved side glass and an extreme tumblehome were crowning touches to a beautiful car. Making a four-door convertible with doors that open from the center is quite an engineering feat. The extremely rigid unit-body structure required no additional reinforcement for the convertible, which weighed 5,220 pounds (2,369.8kg) fully equipped. The convertible top mechanism borrowed extensively from Ford's retractable top, even to the flip-top boot. The rigidity of the body allowed short but strong center pillars, which acted as door locks and kept the doors in line.

Only 212.4 inches (539.5cm) long, the 1961 Continental convertible is one of the greatest open cars ever built. Each Continental was subjected to a twelve-mile (19.2km) road test to iron out any problems before delivery. Following any tightening up or other corrections, the cars went out again for another run. Each car, especially a convertible, was subjected to a very severe water leak test, and the automatic transmission was given a

A B O V E : *If the razor sharp body style of the 1961 Lincoln Continental was elegant, so too was the interior, which eschewed chrome for class. In 1961, 2,857 Continental convertibles were produced out of a total 25,164 units. This trim, classic model continued virtually unchanged through 1967.*

A B O V E R I G H T : *The four-door convertible was unique, the first of its type since the abortive 1951 Frazer Manhattan. Unlike the Frazer, there was enough financing to do the job properly. Windows slid out of sight, and the roof disappeared in much the same way the Ford Retractable's did. The doors opened from the center, allowing easy entry and egress.*

thirty-minute "hot test" after being filled with ultraviolet-sensitive dye. The dye showed up leaks under a black light. These were just a few of the things done to make the Continental as near perfect as possible. Even the 430-cubic-inch (7,046.4 cubic cm), 300-bhp V8 was given a three-hour "hot test" running at ninety-eight mph (156.8kph) for part of the time. Then they were torn down, inspected, and reassembled. Considering the amount of care that went into the Continental, its $6,715 price was a bargain, especially when compared to Rolls-Royce or Bentley. Admittedly, the latter pair went even further with careful construction, but they cost a great deal more than the Continental. The Continental could truthfully claim to belong to that rare, vanishing breed of carefully assembled cars subjected to hand-finishing.

The sixties were an incredible time, not so much for convertibles, but for some of the highest-powered machines ever to take to the road. There was a complete change in automotive thinking, both by public and manufacturers. Cars became more conservative and cleanly styled, led by Bill Mitchell's strong influence at GM. It was a period of change that revolutionized the establishment forever. In 1962, there were finless Chrysler Corporation cars that did little to enhance its sales image. It was Exner's final fling at Chrysler and, with the exception of the Chrysler models, his designs were awkward and unsure. The Windsor was replaced by the 300 series, so named to capitalize on the famed 300 Letter Series, which continued on its own. While the Chrysler Newport 300 and 300H had perhaps the best-looking convertibles since 1957, the same couldn't be said of the downsized Dodge and Plymouth models. Valiant continued without a convertible, as did its Dodge Lancer clone. The model was introduced in 1961, following the Valiant's public acceptance. Big Plymouths and Dodges weren't so big anymore, and bore a strong family resemblance to the Valiant/Lancer pair. Most people hated the Plymouth/Dodge radical long hood, short deck theme, concave grille, and Valiant-style fender line. Actually, the Plymouth Sport Fury and Dodge Polara 500 convertibles were distinctive, quite handsome cars, unlike their awkward-looking hardtop and sedan brothers. They were especially attractive painted white with red trim.

A convertible compact Buick Skylark arrived in 1962, and it had an optional four-speed manual transmission. There was a convertible in Oldsmobile's F-85 compact line, and one for Pontiac's Tempest. This is logical, considering that the three cars shared the same body. Over at Chevrolet, the Corvair introduced a beautiful convertible christened the Monza, which was gorgeous to look at. And there was a new Chevrolet compact called the Chevy II. Rather square but quite appealing, the Chevy II convertible at $2,475 allowed many more to indulge their open-road, over-the-hills fantasies. Face-lifted full-sized cars were ho-hum. The best-looking convertibles were the Buick Electra and Invicta models. Cadillac's sculpturing didn't look right and somehow cheapened the "Standard of the World" and both its convertible models.

Lincoln's Continental convertible remained the epitome of the open road car. Changes were restricted to a cleaner-looking grille. From 1962 to 1967, the Continental went through evolutionary changes, gaining three

Changes were restricted to grille and some trim on the 1964 Lincoln Continental. It was still the most elegant full-size convertible to be found anywhere in the world at that time, a position that was lost after 1967. No more Continental convertibles were built by Lincoln when new styling came in 1968.

inches on its wheelbase (from 123 to 126 [312.4 to 320cm]), and eight inches (20.3cm) in length. There were no more Lincoln convertibles after 1967, thus making the 1961–67 models highly desirable to collectors, who appreciate that this was one of the finest cars ever made in America.

Ford's illustrious Thunderbird was a new, rocket-styled car introduced in 1961, and in 1962, a fiberglass tonneau cover was offered to convert the model into a two-seater. As a sporty car to remind people of the classic two-seater, it didn't work; it was too big. But as an eye-catcher cruising along some balmy sea road, it was tops. A new, cleaner-looking, full-sized Ford came out in 1962. Gone was any trace of fins, and wraparound windshields had disappeared in 1960. Ford stylists had made a complete break with fifties baroque, opting for flat, clean lines across the board. There were 13,183 Sunliner convertibles built, a third of the Galaxie 500XL number.

Despite the 1958 AMA ban on manufacturer participation in auto racing, most continued to do so in an under-the-table manner. Help would be given covertly to racing teams, but it wouldn't be too long before active manufacturer involvement began again. By 1962, it had. Of course, the general public benefited from the racing experience, via better durability, suspension, and handling. As for engines, they grew larger and larger. Maybe it wasn't a good idea to allow inexperienced drivers to walk into a showroom and buy a Sunliner convertible with the optional 406-cubic-inch (6,653.1 cubic cm) V8 and developing 405 brake horses. These engines were great, they were exciting, and they went like rockets. Unfortunately, in the hands of the novice, they could become deathtraps. A high-speed rollover in a convertible gave the driver and passengers as much chance for survival as driving off the Grand Canyon. Be that as it may, big engines were in—and getting bigger, but there were exceptions to the rule.

A new, thin-wall casting technique produced an all-new 221 series small-block V8, which entered service with the new, downsized Ford Fairlanes introduced in 1962. There were no convertibles offered and still none in the popular Falcon series. Six-cylinder power was all that was available in Falcons for 1962, but that would soon change.

American Motors was holding its own very comfortably with a series of sensible cars. The compact American introduced its only convertible in 1961, continuing in 1962. It couldn't be described as the most beautiful, but the American was a well-finished, quality automobile at only $2,344.

Studebaker, on the other hand, was terminally ill. The compact Lark temporarily staved off the inevitable closing of America's oldest auto company. When the Big Three introduced a slew of compacts, Studebaker's

Beautiful evening, beautiful woman, and a beautiful convertible to ride to heaven in. The car, a 1964 ½ Mustang replete with a 289 V-8, is the ideal way to take the escape road to Never Never Land.

days were well and truly numbered. Even the beautiful Brooks Stevens–designed Gran Turismo Hawk, and the radical fiberglass Avanti, mostly designed by Tom Kellogg of Raymond Loewy's studio, were not enough to save Studebaker. In December 1963, the old South Bend, Indiana, plant was closed, and what little production remained was transferred to Hamilton, Ontario, Canada.

Elwood Engel, whom Chrysler snatched away from Ford in mid-1961, got rid of the controversial Exner-designed freestanding headlights on the 1963 Imperial, though he didn't have time to do much about the car itself. The Imperial Crown convertible wasn't the most handsome; on the other hand, the Dodge Polara and new, compact Dodge Dart convert-

ibles were very attractive. Plymouth's Valiant had a new body which was clean-cut and square compared to the stylish 1960–62 model. The all-new Chrysler was horribly awkward, as if one designer had worked on it here, another designer there. In convertible form, it was the least attractive of Chrysler's cars. Nevertheless, Chrysler almost doubled sales over 1962's dismal total, and continued to do well for much of the rest of the decade.

Over at the General's house, Bill Mitchell had been working hard. All full-sized cars lost their sculpturing to be outfitted in clean, square-cut, Ivy League suits. Particularly handsome was Pontiac's new Grand Prix. It was the most graceful-looking Pontiac in years, the total opposite of its predecessors of five years before. But there was no Grand Prix convertible, only a single hardtop. There was a nice-looking Bonneville and a face-lifted Tempest, the latter given a 326 V8 that could do 0-to-60 in under ten seconds. In fact, the convertible was the sporty LeMans offering a luxury interior. Corvette, America's only sports car, was all-new. It became the Corvette Sting Ray, with all-independent suspension, yet still retained drum brakes. In convertible roadster form, powered by the standard 327 V8 available in various degrees of horsepower, the new Corvette was the equal of many European sports cars.

Though this is a book about convertibles, we would be remiss not to mention the stunning Buick Riviera. A mixture of European and American influences, the 1963 Buick Riviera was the car of the decade, and Bill Mitchell's crowning glory. No car, in this author's opinion, was as beautiful or as desirable as the Riviera. It brought elegance back to motoring in a design that has yet to be topped.

Ford's restyled full-sized Galaxie was a beauty in both hardtop and convertible form. Here was a cruiser that looked massive yet elegant at the same time. Interiors were luxurious, and with the right engine, it was powerful. That engine was the hairy 427, though hardly anyone ordered it. The intermediate Fairlane was virtually the same as 1962 and still had no convertible. As for Falcon, there was the new, top-of-the-line Futura series that introduced the Sprint subseries. There were convertibles in four-, five-, and six-passenger guises. (The interior of the first was decked out with four bucket seats.) The four-seat Falcon was trying to steal some of

the Corvair Monza Spyder's thunder, though the Corvair beat it, two to one. Chevy's big Bel-Air and Impala had new bodies that were very stylish, and in convertible form arguably better-looking than the Ford. Still, Chevrolet had a terrific year, producing over 2.3 million units, beating Ford by more than 700,000. Mercury had introduced its compact offering in 1960. Some thought the Comet looked like a Falcon on a dinner date, for it was similar to the lower-priced car. In convertible form, it was quite smart with its stainless steel (chrome) trim and better-finished interior.

In 1963, Lee Iacocca, who had become head of the Ford Division in 1960, pooh-poohed AMA race ban rulings and introduced Ford's Total Performance program. A result of the program was the whopping 406-cubic-inch (6,653.1 cubic cm) V8 developing 405 horsepower. The engine was built to keep up with the bigger and bigger offerings coming out of GM and Chrysler (Chevrolet had the now-famous 409-cubic-inch [6,702.2 cubic cm] and Plymouth a lowly 361-cubic-inch [5,915.7 cubic cm] V8). By 1963, Plymouth

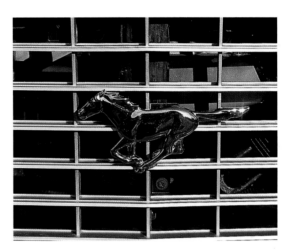

was trouncing the opposition on the tracks, using a Super Stock Wedge V8 displacing 426 cubic inches (6,980.8 cubic cm). Two versions of this wild engine were made available to the public, which could choose between 415 or 425 horsepower. Ford had the awesome 427, though buyers preferred the lesser, but still mighty, 406 V8.

A face-lifted Falcon introduced the sharp Futura and Sprint models. Actually, the Sprint was the upper end of the Futura series. The standard Sprint convertible was a six-passenger car with bench seats, while the Sprint sported four leather-grained vinyl buckets. There was also a five-passenger model with buckets up front and a bench in the rear. Falcon Sprints had the 260 V8 standard; equipped with this engine, it won its class at the prestigious Monte Carlo Rallye. At around $2,800, a Futura Sprint convertible was a little ambitious for youngsters to consider, even those working after school.

There were more minor face-lifts from GM. (Not that convertibles were foremost on corporate minds. A man by the name of Ralph Nader was beginning to make uncomfortable waves concerning the roadability of the Corvair.) In 1964, it was Ford's turn to make real headlines. No, not with bigger engines—there were plenty of those—but with an automotive concept not tried before. On April 17 that year, America woke up to Mustang mania. If Ford got it wrong with the Edsel, they got it right with the Mustang. It was an unprecedented success, selling better than Ford ever dreamed it would.

ABOVE: *Here's a 1964 ½ surrounded by four of its namesakes. Originally the name came up when somebody mentioned the World War II P-51 Mustang fighter plane. Not wanting the car to be associated with violence or war, the notion was dropped. Then somebody said: "What about Mustang ponies?"*

ABOVE RIGHT: *Run wild, run free. That's exactly what Ford wanted people to think when they saw the Mustang galloping across the grille. It worked, too. Over 681,000 Mustangs were produced between 1964 and 1965, and of these, 101,945 were convertibles.*

In 1964, Pontiac quietly introduced the world's first intermediate-bodied muscle car. It debuted as an additional model in the Tempest range and was called the GTO. It had the performance to lay waste to Ferraris in a straight line, though corners were a different story. Shown here is the 1966 restyled GTO, which followed the coke-bottle styling fad of the mid- to late sixties. The biggest engine in the GTO was the 389 cid V-8.

Based upon an idea Lee Iacocca carried around in his little black book for a sporty four-seater about the length of the original two-seater Thunderbird, the Mustang began as a dinner conversation piece at the Fairlane Inn in Dearborn. After a while, the dinner dreams evolved into a practical idea. Iacocca was looking for a mid-1964 launch, necessitating a lot of time to bring the project to fruition. After a couple of false starts, the car's final shape and engineering were finalized. One thing Iacocca insisted upon was a lower-than-low base price of $2,300. Everything the planners set out to do with the concept was achieved. There were three models: a two-door coupé, two-door fastback, and a two-door convertible. A huge

advertising campaign started the week before launch, and every magazine and newspaper carried stories on the Mustang. Dealers couldn't remember a time when a new car generated so much excitement. They were bowled over by the stampede into Ford showrooms; more than four million people visited dealerships during the first weekend.

There was little doubt the Mustang was an extremely pretty car. Designed by Ford studio chief Joe Oros and his talented assistant, Dave Ash, the car was based upon the Falcon floorpan. Eighteen months after design approval, the Mustang was in the showrooms. Quickly labeled a "pony car" by the motoring press, the Mustang was a car for the young at heart. In convertible form, the Mustang was the epitome of youth, exuberance, romance. It was the escape road personified. The base engine was a six-cylinder; the only option at the time was Ford's 260 V8. As with all convertibles, extra strengthening was required: on the hardtop and fastbacks, heavy box-section side rails and five welded crossmembers made up the base. On convertibles, a heavier-gauge steel with reinforcement applied to the rocker panels gave the rigidity required. A soft-top was listed at $2,614, though options such as the V8, bucket seats, limited slip differential, and radio would boost the price well over $3,000. Yet the Mustang became one of the best-selling convertibles in history, with 101,945 produced between 1964 and 1965. Other Fords were restyled, with the convertible Galaxie 500XL one of the best-looking for many years.

The General stuck with much the same styling it had had since 1962, although there were a few significant changes in 1965. Several divisions adopted the "Coke bottle" shape. The design was particularly pleasing in the Chevrolet Impala SS convertible. Even better was the redesigned Corvair; the car was an absolute beauty, with greatly improved road holding and suspension. Radical improvements to the Corvair had been enacted before Ralph Nader's book, *Unsafe At Any Speed*, was published. Cadillac hardly changed; it just appeared to grow longer. A Caddy convertible had squarish styling, reminding one of an aircraft carrier deck. Buick, large Pontiacs, and Oldsmobile had variations of the Coke bottle,

though none as acute as the Impala. Intermediates and compacts kept the square look for another season.

Pontiac set the world on fire when it introduced the intermediate GTO in 1964. With the 348-horse 389 under the hood, the GTO convertible was the fastest around. Recognized as the first true muscle car, the Pontiac GTO beat a Ferrari GTO in a straight line, according to a *Car & Driver* road test. Dodge/Plymouth intermediates, powered by second-generation hemis, beat everybody at NASCAR in 1964 and again in '65. There was a nice Dodge Dart convertible which, equipped with the $99.40 273-cubic-inch (4,473.6 cubic cm) V8, could do 0-to-60 in about eight seconds. The car had front

bucket seats that were attractively trimmed in vinyl, though it looked as if an oval sardine can had been used as inspiration for the taillights.

Chrysler brought out an all-new Imperial styled by Elwood Engel. There was much of Engel's 1961 Continental styling in the car, including the front-to-back chrome cappings and square roofline. Twin grilles distinguished the attractive automobile, which was the best-looking Imperial since 1958.

Elwood Engel's influence on the 1965 Chryslers was very apparent. These were his designs, pure and simple. Long and low, the sculptured sides were accented by his full-length chrome trim at the top belt line. As a convertible—only 440 were made—the last 300 Letter Series high-performance car, the 300L, left the stage somewhat diluted from its original concept. Indeed, it had a high output 413 V8 to distance it from the regular 300 line (it used a 383), and the interior had distinctive appointments. Other than that, there were no differences, so it had to be a car buff who knew you were driving a special convertible into the golf club parking lot.

Once again, Ford was completely restyled in 1965. Square lines followed the theme set by Thunderbird's new design in 1964. Vertical dual headlights and a grille made up of thin horizontal bars expressed the simple but direct approach to the car's design. It was quite the opposite of late-fifties Ford styling. The top convertible continued to be the five-passenger Galaxie 500XL. The interiors were very attractive, with a floor-mounted shift lever to add to the sporty look. V8s up to 427 cubic inches (6,997.2 cubic cm) gave the sporty look a very sporty drive—in a straight

ABOVE: *The 1966 GTO interior was as sporty as it was handsome, even if the so-called wood-rimmed steering wheel was a fake. At least it managed to look the part. Very fast and with excellent handling, the GTO convertible was on the right track to Valhalla.*

ABOVE RIGHT: *Stacked headlights were used by the GTO only in 1966 and 1967. A new design in 1968 found the duals horizontal again. The 1966 GTO looked just right with the vertical lights, which complemented Pontiac's traditional twin grilles.*

Chevrolet's Corvette got a complete redesign in 1968 and seven inches (17.8cm) in extra length. The 98-inch (248.9cm) wheelbase remained the same. Critics weren't too keen on the new Corvette, stating it was overweight and clumsy by European comparisons. It was extremely fast, nonetheless. Improvements were made to the car during its 14-year cycle (a 1969 version is shown), but it wasn't until the eighties that Corvette could hold its head up as a true sports car capable of taking on the world.

line, of course! Mercury sported a big Park Lane convertible stuffed with everything but the kitchen sink. Like Ford, the Mercury had square lines and "Torque Box" body construction. This meant each model's frame was tuned to reduce vibration, harshness, and noise.

American Motors' first full line of convertibles was quite an event. There was the compact American 440, Classic 770, and the ultraluxurious Ambassador 990. Designed by Dick Teague, AMC called its cars the "Sensible Spectaculars." They were sensible and very attractive and should have done much better than the 12,334 units they sold for the combined three marques.

Although there were convertibles in 1966, there was nothing really distinguishable about them. Ford added convertibles to its growing lineup of Fairlane intermediate models, but overall there appeared to be slackening of interest in romantic wind-in-your-hair motoring in favor of the escalating blood 'n' guts machismo offered by the lightweight intermediates with racing engines under the hoods. A seven-liter (1.8g) engine was

considered marginally safer in a hardtop than in a convertible. The big automotive news for 1966 was Oldsmobile's beautiful Toronado hardtop coupé. It was the first American front-wheel drive car since the troubled Cord of 1937. The Toronado was also the longest and heaviest FWD (front-wheel drive) car ever built. It was engineering at its best.

The muscle car wars of 1968–69 were so intense that hardly anything else was written about in automobile magazines. A slick-looking Dodge Dart could run 0-to-60 in six seconds, a hemi-powered Dodge Charger flew to sixty in a mere 4.8 seconds. Remember, these were cars straight off the showroom floor. Even the convertibles were quick. A Dodge Coronet R/T convertible loaded with a 440 V8 was able to run to sixty in 6.6 seconds, maybe faster, depending which way the wind was blowing. Bearing in mind the 135 mph (216kph) top speed, the Coronet would have had to

have a lot of strength. All unitized car bodies rely on pseudo-frame structures that are longitudinal members. These are an integral part of the floorpan-body sill structure. Additional strength is applied with sheet metal ribs that are welded into the central cavity of the sill box section. The ribs run full length, resulting in greater torsional rigidity. Additional reinforcement is often built into the cowl structure of a convertible, thus contributing further to the safety of this type of car.

Psychedelic was the name of the game by 1967. Even the car companies took note of this phenomenon. They began couching their advertising copy in psychedelic metaphors that only the young could understand. It

was all escape; the young wanted to escape the horrors Vietnam had brought to home and show their parents they didn't share the same values. Besides advertising copy, the cars adopted outrageous colors. Plum Crazy, Tangerine Orange, and Lemon Twist were just a few. Plymouth took the psychedelic thing to heart in 1969. Besides the outrageous advertising, there was even a Barracuda decked out with garish floral patterned seats and a flower power vinyl roof!

There were a few interesting convertibles in the final years of the Swinging Sixties. Chevrolet and Pontiac's answers to Ford's Mustang were two

of them. Attractively styled and very fast with the right engine and suspension combinations, Chevrolet's Camaro and Pontiac's Camaro clone, the Firebird, had convertibles that fit the "over the hills and far away" image. For some reason, pony cars didn't bother the hippie youth cult; they pursued traditional values so long as the local sheriff didn't see them burn rubber on a quiet back country road.

Thanks to safety advocate Ralph Nader and insurance companies alarmed by the power under the pedal of many cars, the federal government took steps to rectify the situation. Cars had to be safe, Detroit was warned, otherwise there might be trouble. Lap and shoulder belts, already common in Europe, collapsible steering columns, side impact reinforcement, chassis reinforcement, energy-absorbing front ends, five mph (8kph) crash bumpers—Detroit and Dearborn had their work cut out. Side marker lights appeared in 1968, and other safety features quickly followed. But the motor industry had lost its way; one of the most turbulent decades of the century came to an end, but nobody was sure about the future.

Chapter 6

VANISHING POINT AND BEYOND

Compared to four-door sedans, convertibles had always been nonstarters. Everybody loved convertibles and many dreamed of owning one, but comparatively few ever did. Convertibles cost more and were not considered people-haulers. Manufacturers made their money from the old reliable family hack: four doors, lots of room, and a roof. But the convertible was an image-builder, an enticement into the showroom. And you can be sure Motown never lost money on convertibles.

Obviously, convertible concentrations are more common in the Sun Belt areas such as California, Florida, Arizona, and New Mexico, and least likely in the Midwest, where the climate

is very inhospitable. In 1965, the American auto industry produced 509,419 convertibles, or 5.48 percent of total auto production. By 1970, this had sagged to a dismal 91,863 (1.40 percent), and in 1974 a puny 27,955 (0.50 percent). Why the drastic decline? Probably a combination of events.

Vietnam, for one: America's young men didn't know when their number would be called to go to this hellhole. Then there were all the possible convertible buyers killed in Vietnam; the growing safety awareness; and, perhaps most important of all, the imported car. Detroit was digging its own grave with lackluster workmanship and old hat technology. Why pay $5,000 for a convertible when there was a smaller, fuel efficient, reliable European car for half the money? Then there was a new threat from Japan. Nobody thought much of the embryonic forms driving off freighters into Pacific ports, but soon they would multiply and expand until they became as much a part of the American auto industry as American cars themselves.

Despite the growing public disillusionment, Detroit still offered some interesting convertibles in 1970. Plymouth's Barracuda had all-new styling that emphasized the long-hood, short-deck fashion prevalent at the time. Plymouth offered more models in three series—there was only one in 1969—beginning with the base Barracuda. In the middle was the Gran Coupé, and at the top the very racy 'Cuda. Nine engine combinations were also available. Each series had a convertible, the best being the 'Cuda version. Plymouth's Barracuda got a kissin' cousin when Dodge—somewhat belatedly—entered the pony car field with the Challenger. It shared much with the Barracuda, but rode on a wheelbase two inches (5.0cm) longer (110 inches [279.4cm]). Like the Barracuda, the Challenger offered a range of engines starting with a straight-six and ending with a rip-roaring 426 hemi V8 and a 440 wedge. Certainly, the top engine for both Barracuda and Challenger pony cars was the 340. Built for racing, the 340

ABOVE TOP: *Natty pleated cloth and vinyl seating is complemented by a business-like dash with a full range of instruments in 1970 the Mustang Boss 351. A number of engine options were deleted after 1970, including the 428. Only three were offered in 1972.*

ABOVE BOTTOM: *Mustang displayed its power on either side of the Shaker hood scoop. Low gloss black paint decorates the hood with wide and narrow stripes.*

RIGHT: *The engine bay of the Boss 351 is quite crowded, making it difficult to work on. The last year for the famous Cleveland 351 V-8 was 1973; after that, Mustang IIs' largest engine was the 302.*

was well balanced and very fast. Both cars competed in the popular Trans Am competition dominated by Mustang and Camaro. There were 1,070 convertible Challengers made in 1970, compared to 2,785 Barracudas of all derivatives. This contrasts markedly with the 11,354 Oldsmobile Cutlass Supreme convertibles built, which could be had with the big 455 engine. The standard engine was the tried and true 350 V8. Whatever the motor, the 1970–71 Cutlass had poise, managing to look civilized even when laying rubber along the midnight cool tarmac.

A unique American phenomenon, the muscle car, the envy of boy racers the world over, had had its day. It was doomed, the victim of high insurance rates, safety regulations, and slackening public interest. Ragtop cars, muscle-bound or otherwise, were on the way out. It was a pity, because 1970–71 afforded some interesting machines.

There was the 1970 Plymouth Road Runner, which handled and drove like a thoroughbred, and the pretty 1971 Mercury Cougar, which was more a cruiser than a handler. Cadillac's front-wheel drive Eldorado was redesigned for 1971 and included a convertible. Some called it baroque—it looked a bit like a rotund painted lady from an eighteenth-century boudoir—especially if it had white paint, white interior, and white top. Besides being a bit overwhelming in the looks department, the Eldorado boasted the world's largest engine: 8.2 liter [2.1g] (500 cubic inches [8,193.5 cubic cm]) and 400 horsepower. This enormous engine was standard only on the Eldorado, which, bearing the car in mind, seemed appropriate.

Struggling to meet government edicts for emissions and safety, the Big Three lost their way in terms of design and quality, thereby opening the floodgates to an automotive invasion from Japan in the late seventies. A dull period set in and the cars became less individual, as the companies tried badge engineering to save money. Muscle cars were relegated to go-faster stripes and a once-proud name, and almost all convertibles were dispensed

with by 1973, the year of the oil crisis. Ford dropped all open-top models in 1972, the last being the 1971 intermediate Torino. At least it went out with a bang if the buyer ordered the optional 429 V8. The beloved Mustang and Mercury Cougar kept up appearances until 1973. Mustang almost doubled its convertible sales in 1973, with 11,853 units built com-

By the mid-eighties the American automobile was generally smaller, lighter, and more fuel-efficient than its earlier counterparts. The 1987 Pontiac Sunbird was a good-looking, small front-wheel-drive convertible with enough romantic pizzazz to take the open top escape road to the sun. The Sunbird above is the GT with the 2-liter OHC 4-cylinder, turbocharged engine rated at 165 bhp.

pared to 6,401 the previous year. Dodge and Plymouth called it a day and built their last convertibles in 1970, but Buick gritted its teeth, continuing to offer a LeSabre ragtop through 1976. Chevrolet had a Caprice Classic convertible until 1976, perhaps thinking if Ford and Plymouth no longer made them, then it would satisfy the demand. Not that the demand was much: 31,667 units from 1972 to 1975. Who's to say convertible sales might have been less had Ford and Plymouth continued making them?

There was a great hullabaloo in 1976: Cadillac announced the end of America's last surviving convertible. Production, Cadillac told us, would be fourteen thousand units. Suddenly, people became aware that an era was fast coming to an end—no more convertibles. Buyers telephoned, they wrote letters, they lined up. They all wanted the last convertible. Cadillac rubbed its hands in glee, confidently predicting it would sell the entire fourteen thousand. Just to stir up the fever a little more, Cadillac

announced that there would be a limited run of two hundred special Eldorado convertibles. They were to be white on white on white—you could almost say albino. Even the hubcaps were white. The white leather was rich and buttoned and the chrome was real chrome, not the plastic variety fast coming into vogue. And there was a special dash plaque commemorating "the end of an era."

Demand was so great for the two hundred Special Edition models, Cadillac could have sold them ten times over and there still wouldn't have been enough to sate the appetite for these cars. All Eldorado convertibles were sold, the two hundred specials doubling their prices overnight. Speculators ran rampant, some paying almost $30,000 for a $12,000 car, confident they would double their money again within months. Cadillac car clubs and other motoring organizations warned it wouldn't happen, but nobody listened. Like all seven-day wonders, prices peaked at $30,000, then dropped like a stone when people realized the almost identical 1975 Eldorado convertible was fifty percent less common than the hyped '76. Instant collectibles are rarely collectible, yet people are gullible enough to be taken in every time somebody offers a limited edition this or that.

ABOVE: *Chrysler launched the decade's instant legend when it allowed Dodge to produce the mighty V-10 Viper. The Viper's incredible styling is all sports, with no gimmicks. In 1992, the Viper was a roadster, not a convertible because it did not have roll-up windows.*

ABOVE RIGHT: *The Viper's center console has a six-speed shift lever and parking brake. Black on white round instruments are featured on the dashboard. Extras are few and far between; there is no radio, for instance. All that matters is the driving experience.*

OPPOSITE: *After years in the doldrums, Chrysler came back with a bang, thanks to Lee Iacocca. In the nineties Chrysler stole a march on everybody with its smart "cab-forward" styling. A six-speed transmission services the all-aluminum V-10 engine, which is alarmingly quick.*

This is exactly what happened with the Eldorado, a car nobody wants or cares about. That was it. No more convertibles. Detroit's cars muddled along with poor styling and poor quality throughout the seventies, a decade many considered the most barren of the century.

Chrysler entered 1980 in worse shape than usual. The great auto company was virtually bankrupt, with no salvation in sight. Then came a miracle in the name of Lee Iacocca. Father of the Mustang and Ford's good fortunes until Henry Ford II suddenly dismissed him, Iacocca took the job of putting Chrysler back on its feet. First, he negotiated a multibillion dollar loan of taxpayers' money, then prepared the way for Chrysler's new, downsized front-wheel drive K-cars. From Chrysler to Plymouth, most components were shared on what was known as the K-car platform. A massive advertising campaign was launched, with Iacocca appearing  in many of the TV commercials. Soon he became a household word, and Chrysler got up on its feet and began to make profits again. Chrysler did so well with the K-cars that Iacocca was able to repay the government loan back in full, well before the debt was due.

It was a revived Chrysler that introduced two of the first convertibles to be seen for many years. There was the 1982 Chrysler LeBaron convertible, sporting a luxury interior and a 2.2-liter (8.3L) Trans-4 engine with a four-speed manual transaxle. The only engine option was a Mitsubishi-built 2.6-liter (9.8L) overhead-cam four. The Dodge convertible was basically the same. Both cars were converted from the coupé by Cars & Concepts of Brighton, Michigan. Cars & Concepts also did a Buick Riviera convertible, which came out the same time as the Chrysler models.

In 1984, Cadillac brought back the Eldorado convertible, much to the chagrin of those who were sitting on 1976 Eldorados in the hopes they would make a killing. But the 1984 version was as different from the 1976s as chalk is from cheese. For one thing, it had all-independent suspension and much improved front-wheel drive. Loaded to the gills, the 1984 Eldorado was as tasteful as its 1976 predecessor wasn't. It also cost nearly three times as much, at $32,000. Chrysler dipped into the nostalgia barrel in 1984 and came up with a new Chrysler Town & Country convertible, complete with plastic wood sides. Still, at $16,300, it was a smart car in which to go places.

In 1985, Dodge added a turbocharger to its 600 convertible. Performance, it seemed, was making a comeback. Chevrolet rejoined the convertible club in 1983 with the compact front-wheel drive Cavalier. At the same time, Ford returned to ragtop models when it added one to its Mustang lineup. This is still Ford's only convertible to date, with the exception of the diminutive Australian-built Mercury Capri, introduced in 1990 and dropped in 1994.

Following in Chevy's footsteps, Pontiac had its own convertible on the same J-car platform. When it first appeared in 1983, it was the 2000; later it became the Sunbird. It had the same sluggish 2.0-liter (0.5g) four-cylinder engine, and, though the traditional twin grilles were distinctive, the rest of the car was identical to the Cavalier. So what? Both cars were convertibles, and any convertible was better than no convertible at all.

After the dowdy seventies, America's automobile industry did an about-face in the eighties, bringing out cars that made the previous decade's technology depressingly antiquated. Scared into action by the

aggressive Japanese, Ford led the way with its magnificent and aerodynamic Taurus, introduced in 1985. Meanwhile, Chrysler brought out the Plymouth Voyager and Dodge Caravan minivans. A completely new concept in people-carriers, the twin minivans took off like wildfire. As for convertibles, it was much the same as before. American car-makers, like the

Europeans, had long shelved ideas of new cars every year. No longer did cars have major restyling; rather, they looked the same each year, but benefitted from continual improvement.

Cadillac came out with the ultimate convertible in 1987. This was the sporty two-seater Allante, an incredible machine designed by Pininfarina in Italy. Pininfarina built the bodies in Italy and shipped them by air to

ABOVE: *1992 was the last year for the third-generation Pontiac Firebird/Trans Am series, which had sold almost three quarters of a million units since its introduction ten years earlier. Considering its front engine, rear drive, and solid rear axle layout, Pontiac's ponycar was very good indeed. Crammed with luxury as well as sparkling performance, the Trans Am reminds one of the sort of car the Saint or James Bond might allow themselves to be seen driving.*

TOP LEFT: *Here is the heart of the Pontiac Firebird/Trans Am: the 5.7 liter unit developing 235 bhp (net), and a strong heart it is, too. There were three 5.0L and a 3.1L V-6 to choose from, but the fuel-injected 5.7L V-8 was capable of performing to the max.*

BOTTOM LEFT: *The rear view of the Pontiac Firebird-Trans Am '92 shows a distinct wedge shape. Wheels are gold anodized and perhaps a little too decorative for the car.*

Shiny chrome wheels highlight the racy yellow limited edition special convertible Mustang that was built in 1993. Only 1,419 were built, and they were all yellow. Ford's venerable 5.0L V-8 was under the hood. Though it seemed to have been around since Moses was discovered in the bullrushes, it was a great engine, nonetheless. As can be seen, the 1993 Limited Edition was a great way to let the sun shine in, and it was Ford's way of saying goodbye to fourteen years of friendship.

Detroit for completion. At a heart-tugging $54,000, the 1987 Allante wasn't for everybody, yet Cadillac confidently expected to sell four thousand in its first year. In fact, only 1,651 Allantes found homes. It was a very exclusive kind of car. Powered by Cadillac's 4.1-liter (1g) transverse-mounted V8 with multiport fuel injection, the Allante had good performance and road-holding. Initially, the car had a lot of problems, such as a manual top (after paying the high price, buyers expected a power top),

gimmicky gauges that looked cheap, fittings identical to those found on lesser cars, a ride that was too firm, an under-powered engine (which was fixed when the Northstar V8 replaced the original engine), and overall poor quality. By the time Cadillac had ironed out all the problems, the car was axed.

But all through the years, America's only sports car maker, Corvette, offered ragtops. There was a break in the seventies, and it wasn't until

1986 that the Corvette once again had a convertible. It was a very quick convertible, perhaps one of the fastest in the world, even more so in 1987 when horsepower climbed to 240 (net). Dodge gave up its convertible in 1987, while the Chrysler LeBaron received an all-new body. At the same time, Pontiac's Sunbird got a face-lift and a natty two-tone paint job that made the car quite attractive. With a 165 hp (net) turbocharged engine, the Sunbird was definitely very sporty. A special limited edition Mustang convertible was offered to celebrate the marque's twentieth anniversary in 1989. The 5.0-liter (1.3g), V8-powered car came in a deep emerald green metallic clearcoat, and had a white top and leather interior. Cadillac continued with its Allante, which remained the same but cost $3,000 more, and Chevrolet's Camaro IROC Z-28 gave those nostalgic for front engine and rear drive all they needed. Though it and its virtual twin, the Pontiac Trans Am, had modern technology rooted with the old, both cars were the sixties once more.

In the nineties there was a more aggressive, greedy, and violent ambience in the air, courtesy of Hollywood. The auto market reflected the new mood with a tremendous upswing in pickup truck and utility vehicle sales. However, minivans and cars continued to do well in a market where an annual production total of under fourteen million units was considered a recession! Foreign cars held twenty-five percent of America's automobile market in 1990, even though the nation was building the best cars it had made in years. Convertibles continued on the market, but only in small doses. Buick offered a convertible in its limited production sports-type Reatta. There were 2,200 built, each costing a little over $35,000.

A 1995 Chevrolet Camaro purrs along Interstate 8 through Arizona into California with its top up, which is a good idea when traveling the Southwest in 110 degree heat. Whatever the conditions, the Camaro takes it all in its stride.

The Reatta was dropped after 1992, and Buick hasn't bothered with a convertible since.

American and Japanese car companies, rather than fight each other, decided to form joint partnerships: Mazda and Ford (the Probe is built by Mazda at its factory in Michigan) teamed up; Suzuki and Toyota joined forces with Chevrolet to build the successful Geo line; and Chrysler has a strong relationship with Mitsubishi. Whatever some might say, this sort of cooperation can only improve the automobiles we drive, as each partner learns from the other. Convertibles, unfortunately, continued to take a back seat to almost everything on wheels. Pickups, utilities, and minivans continued their upward spiral as they became more and more sophisticated. Standard two- and four-door cars were full of high tech and computer chips, refined air conditioning, and sound systems the envy of concert halls, so a convertible was no longer the romantic conveyance it once was. Urban sprawl and runaway development had taken their toll in the areas where the convertible came into its own. Driving through residential developments at 15 mph (24kph) or down overcrowded thoroughfares lined with fast-food places is not romantic or free. In a few places in our shrinking country there are spots where one can drive without seeing another vehicle, building, or person. Arizona, Montana, and New Mexico fit the bill for top-down, open-road adventure. But what is left as we hit the second half of the nineties?

One of the most enduring and popular convertibles in recent years has been Chrysler's LeBaron. Since its inception in 1982, the LeBaron has sold very well (52,338 produced in 1989; 45,975 in 1990), but by 1994 it was getting a bit long in the tooth. Late in 1992, Chrysler introduced the much vaunted LH series of "cab-forward" cars. There were three: the Chrysler Concorde, Eagle Vision, and Dodge Intrepid. In one stroke, just as it did in 1957, Chrysler stole the styling march on the rest of the industry with cars that not only looked good, but had state-of-the-art technology to match. There were no convertibles; only the old LeBaron soldiered on, having gone as far as it could on its K-car platform. In 1995, Chrysler introduced two smaller cab-forward cars, the Chrysler Cirrus and Dodge Stratus. Then came the Mitsubishi-built Chrysler Sebring, a very impressive machine. In the summer of 1995, Chrysler introduced the Sebring convertible as a 1996 model; it replaced the aging LeBaron. Only the convertible wasn't built by Mitsubishi. It was entirely different from Mitsubishi based upon the Cirrus/Stratus platform, yet it was built at a Chrysler plant in Mexico. There are two models, the base JX and the JXi. The former has a 150-horsepower 2.4-liter (0.6g) V4, and the more expensive JXi has a 2.5-liter (0.6g) V6 made by Mitsubishi that develops 163 horses. Four-wheel disc brakes and antilock are standard on the JXi, as are dual airbags. A nice touch is the standard power-operated folding top, which includes a glass rear window and defroster. It's a supercar designed to go into the next century in style.

A 2.4-liter (0.6g) double overhead-cam (dohc) four-cylinder engine christened the Twin-Cam, four-speed automatic, traction control, antilock brakes, driver and passenger airbags, air conditioning—these are a few of the standard items on Chevrolet's 180-inch-long (457.2cm) Cavalier.

This 1996 Mustang GT is parked near the dunes just west of Yuma, Arizona. This design replaced the previous model in 1994 and has been a strong seller ever since. The crease along the sides harkens back to the first Mustang, and the latest model is just as distinctive. It is extremely fast and very sophisticated compared to its first-generation brethren.

There is a look of the Dodge Neon in the styling, which is to be expected, considering the Chrysler product beat out everyone else when it came out. Regrettably, the Neon doesn't have a convertible like the Cavalier. With the Twin-Cam engine, the Cavalier takes off briskly and can be even brisker if the five-speed manual transmission is specified. Though not a tear-away machine like the Camaro or illustrious Corvette convertibles, the Cavalier is a good way to go for a young couple not yet saddled with a million responsibilities.

Though it looks a little different, Pontiac's Sunfire convertible is essentially the same as the Cavalier. Likewise the Firebird, which is very similar to the Camaro. In Trans Am guise, Pontiac's pony car is extremely quick, but no fun in the wet. Far better traction can be found in the Corvette, which is a world-class thoroughbred sports car meant to be driven. Ford has only one convertible in its entire fleet, and that is the Mustang. After fifteen years in the same suit of clothes, the Mustang was totally redesigned for 1994, though the engine and mechanics remained much the same. In the 5.0-liter (1.3g) GT guise, the Mustang could hold its own against others of its ilk, although there wasn't much it could do about the aggressive Dodge Viper. In 1996, a limited edition Cobra version was put onto the street. It came both as a white coupé and convertible, and had Ford's modular V8 engine to take it to almost 150 mph (240kph).

As we head into the twenty-first century, the question arises: will there be any convertibles left after the year 2000? There are only seven American ones at present, a far cry from the numbers produced in the fifties and sixties. Europe and Japan build a few more, but the total is not earthshaking. With America looking more and more like an overcrowded anthill, those

who dream of long rides with the top down will have to find new spaces. Developers haven't ruined Arizona or New Mexico yet, and they are the perfect places to drive, while looking like Barry Newman in the 1970 road movie classic, *Vanishing Point*, or the two easy-come, easy-go TV lads who used to travel the old, lamented Route 66 in their Corvette.

Convertible travel is not something to dream about while sitting in your armchair. It is still possible to do. Take off with your loved one and share this most exhilarating experience. Drive that convertible into the sun, over the hills, and far, far away. When you return, you will have shared the magic only a convertible can give you, an emotion you will never forget. Go for it!

ABOVE: *The rear view of the Viper convertible coupé. It is one of the first such models to be sold; an English pop musician bought it. Painted in American racing colors, this Viper could hold its own against almost all of the world's sports cars.*

OPPOSITE: *James Bond's famous creator, Ian Fleming, used to live in the house behind the 1996 Viper. Nestled beneath the White Cliffs of Dover, the house faces across the English Channel to France: an excellent setting for the brooding Viper to be in. One can imagine 007 running out of the house and jumping in the Viper to take part in another adventure of world-saving derring-do.*

Index

Photo Credits

All photography by Nicky Wright

All photography taken with Pentax 6 x 7, Pentax 645,
and Nikon cameras.Fuji film was used throughout.